CU00726621

PLAN
YOUR
CAREER

Also in the Career PowerTools Series

PLAN YOUR CAREER

JOHN LOCKETT

ORION BUSINESS
BOOKS

First published in Great Britain in 1999 by
Orion Business
An imprint of The Orion Publishing Group Ltd
Orion House
5 Upper St Martin's Lane
London WC2H 9EA

A CIP catalogue record for this book
is available from the British Library.

ISBN 0–75282–079–6

Typeset by Deltatype Ltd, Birkenhead
Printed and bound in Great Britain
by Clays Ltd, St Ives plc.

CONTENTS

Part four WHAT SKILLS WILL YOU NEED?

Part five ACTION PLANNING

INTRODUCTION

In the last few years the world of work has changed. It has become less secure, more volatile and a lot less predictable. Everyone is talking about downsizing, delayering and managing change as well as other trends such as globalisation and the power of the Internet, all of which change the way we do business. You may find these exciting times or you may feel anxious about the future – either way, you know that the world of work has changed forever.

If the world of work has changed, then so too has the way in which you manage your career. Changing times need a changing response and this book looks at the key things you need to do and know in order to manage your career in the future. The game has changed and so have the rules. Managing your career is one of your most important priorities for the future. It is most definitely your responsibility and no one else's – certainly the days of your employer managing your career are over. Employers can give you support and guide your development, but only you can decide what is the best career move for you and how you want your career to grow and develop in the future.

The fact that you are reading this book indicates that your career is very important to you. You may be facing some career crisis, or just feel that managing your own career is likely to be much more satisfying than letting it be managed either by your own organisation or just by the seductive looking job adverts that appear in the newspapers or professional journals. Managing your career is, like parenthood, a job for life – the world of work is too turbulent and unpredictable to leave your career development to chance at any stage, whether you are a graduate trainee or two or three years from retirement.

Plan Your Career is divided into five parts. The first four aim to guide you through the stages of successful career planning, while the fifth provides an action plan based on the golden rules of career planning that you will find throughout the book.

It is up to you to tailor the lessons in this book to suit your particular employment situation, but whatever that situation might be, you will find within these pages the help and guidance you need to begin to proactively manage your career, giving you the skills necessary to maximise your potential in your working environment.

Part one

WHERE ARE YOU NOW?

Ever since Socrates explained that the 'unexamined life was not worth living' philosophers and psychologists have been encouraging us to know ourselves better. This is particularly important in managing your career, where a clear understanding of your capabilities and values is a valuable guide to your future career direction.

Career success is normally found at the intersection of your skills and your work values. You will be much more productive in a role where you feel confident and competent and which is consistent with the things that you want to achieve at work. Dissonance between skills, values and the role you are playing leads ultimately to stress and career derailment. Of course, many people survive in a state of dissonance but they are always aware that they are not following their real desires or fulfilling their true potential. They settle for second best. The *Career PowerTools* series is for people who want to fulfil their real potential and to enjoy a truly stimulating career.

Managing your career is not only about making job choices, it involves developing new capabilities, increasing your contribution to your organisation and increasing your personal effectiveness, applying your talents and effort to the right things. This part of the book will help you carry out a review of your skills and motivation.

....

UNDERSTANDING YOUR WORK VALUES AND MOTIVATION

This issue is fundamental to our working lives. Many people go through their whole career and never ask themselves what they are working for. Many years ago, working people had fewer choices and so followed their father's profession, or at least did what their parents thought they should do. Following father into the bank, the law, the army or the church was a common trend, and once established in the profession it was difficult to break out and do something different.

Now we live in a world with far more choices, and yet many people are trapped in a job that doesn't meet their aspirations and is inconsistent with their real values and motivation to work. That may be due to inertia or fear of the unknown, but the reasons why people work are often buried quite deep in their subconscious and so require some careful digging, often with the aid of a skilled helper.

This section will help to uncover some of your work values and help to address why you work and what you want to achieve from your work. Psychologists have spent many years trying to identify what motivates people at work, seeking a broad global explanation. The answer is, however, more likely to be found within each individual. Each of us seeks to find our own meaning for our work which others will not necessarily share. Our great task at work is to find what that meaning is for us.

GOLDEN RULE 1

Successful career planning begins with understanding your skills and motivations.

What are your work values?

The following exercise will help you discover the values that underpin your working life and the important things that motivate you.

This questionnaire consists of several pairs of statements contrasted with each other. For each question, decide the alternative that is more important for you and your work values and tick the relevant box. You may find it difficult to identify the one which is the more representative of your true values, but try to tick one of the statements. There are no right or wrong answers and nobody else need see what you do. The questions may help you to resolve some issues about values and your motivation at work.

WORK VALUE QUESTIONNAIRE

I prefer:
1. A: ☐ Developing my talents to their fullest potential

   B: ☐ Displaying a willingness to take charge of a situation

2. A: ☐ Creating an enterprise of my own

   B: ☐ Planning a financially secure future

3. A: ☐ Supporting people who are less fortunate than me

   B: ☐ Striking a balance between work and other activities

4. A: ☐ Pioneering and piloting new activities

   B: ☐ Being respected for my knowledge and expertise

5. A: ☐ Being recognised as successful

   B: ☐ Being well rewarded for the work I do

6. A: ☐ Influencing the way things are done

   B: ☐ Becoming an established authority within my profession or industry

7. A: ☐ Doing things in my own way

   B: ☐ Taking risks to create excellent results

8. A: ☐ Having a well-organised career plan

   B: ☐ Achieving things outside work

9. A: ☐ Providing a service for others

   B: ☐ Solving complex problems

10. A: ☐ Focusing on the task in hand

    B: ☐ Achieving high financial rewards

11. A: ☐ Gaining the respect of others

    B: ☐ Understanding the needs and values of others

12. A: ☐ Having a wide range of interests

    B: ☐ Enjoying significant perks as part of my remuneration package

13. A: ☐ Managing my own career development

    B: ☐ Contributing to the wider community

14. A: ☐ Using my special skills and talents

    B: ☐ Having a better standard of living than my peers

15. A: ☐ Making an impact on other people

    B: ☐ Planning and organising for the future

16. A: ☐ Spending time with friends and family

    B: ☐ Setting stretching goals for myself

17. A: ☐ Taking the lead in a situation

    B: ☐ Initiating new projects and products/services

18. A: ☐ Freedom to choose my work methods and schedules

    B: ☐ Remaining within my chosen profession

19. A: ☐ Making things happen at work

    B: ☐ Being useful to others

20. A: ☐ Developing my individual talents

    B: ☐ Acting as a member of a team

21. A: ☐ Identifying with my organisation

    B: ☐ Actively competing with others within my sector or profession

22. A: ☐ Acquiring higher levels of status within an organisation

    B: ☐ Receiving compensation based on my performance

23. A: ☐ Working hard to be successful

    B: ☐ Dealing with issues that others have not been able to solve

24. A: ☐ Gaining credibility within my organisation

    B: ☐ Contributing to the welfare of others

25. A: ☐ Managing a team of people

    B: ☐ Leading a balanced lifestyle

26. A: ☐ Gaining recognition for my achievements

    B: ☐ Finding space to make my own decisions

27. A: ☐ Making the world a better place

    B: ☐ Creating a pool of money to make better savings and investments

28. A: ☐ Seeking out difficult or challenging projects

    B: ☐ Gaining an equity stake in my organisation

29. A: ☐ Making myself indispensable to my current employer

    B: ☐ Gaining a reputation as an authority in my chosen field

30. A: ☐ Focusing on achieving a noble purpose

    B: ☐ Developing my professional expertise further

31. A: ☐ Persuading people to put my ideas into action

    B: ☐ Pulling off an almost impossible task

32. A: ☐ Creating something new through my own efforts

    B: ☐ Finding more leisure time to pursue my other interests

33. A: ☐ Seeking opportunities to do something in my own way

    B: ☐ Creating enough wealth to retire early

34. A: ☐ Seeking opportunities for promotion and development

    B: ☐ Integrating my work and family responsibilities with other activities

35. A: ☐ Becoming well known for my achievements

    B: ☐ Identifying opportunities to write or research in my chosen field

36. A: ☐ Enjoying everything that life has to offer

    B: ☐ Being able to work within my chosen field

When you have completed the questionnaire, transfer your responses to the appropriate box in the grid below and count your scores for each dimension, placing the total in the final column.

This is not a psychometric test; it is an indicator of the priorities that you set for your values in relation to your work and career. The questionnaire is deliberately designed to force you to make choices between different statements and so the results may be more skewed than you would normally expect.

Look at the two or three highest scores and the lowest scores. You may have one particularly strong dimension which will clearly be an important motivator for you or perhaps there will be two or three dimensions which when put together will more clearly explain your values. Also, there may be one or two dimensions in which you have a particularly low score – this does not mean that they are completely unimportant to you but you probably see them as a lower priority than the others.

Interpreting your score

✎ Write down your dimension scores in the grid provided, in order of priority from first (highest score) to ninth (lowest score).

Dimension										Dimension Score ↓
Achievement	1A	5A	11A	20A	23A	26A	34A	35A		
Task focus	1B	6A	10A	15A	17A	19A	25A	31A		
Autonomy	2A	7A	13A	17B	18A	26B	32A	33A		
Security	2B	8A	15B	20B	21A	22A	24A	29A		
Altruism	3A	9A	11B	13B	19B	24B	27B	30A		
Balance	3B	8B	12A	16A	25B	32B	34B	36A		
Challenge	4A	7B	9B	16B	21B	23B	28A	31B		
Expertise	4B	6B	14A	18B	29B	30B	35B	36B		
Financial	5B	10B	12B	14B	22B	27B	28B	33B		

Dimension	Score

The implications of the dimensions are as follows:

Achievement

Your score on the achievement dimension reflects your commitment to career success by fulfilling your potential and gaining recognition in the eyes of your colleagues. If your score for this is high it demonstrates a strong drive for career success, which may be a positive factor, although taken to extremes it may indicate a desire for fame and reward at the expense of real task achievement.

Task focus

Task focus is an indicator of the importance of leadership and translating ideas into reality through personal impact, leadership and the effective management of people. A high score demonstrates the importance of getting things done and making a contribution; taken to extremes it may indicate a compulsion to take charge and run things.

Autonomy

The autonomy score indicates your need for independence and to take charge of your own destiny. Where this is high it will probably indicate a more entrepreneurial drive and a desire to work as an independent entity. If very high, it may indicate a high degree of detachment and discomfort with any pressure to conform to organisational norms.

Security

The security dimension measures your need to be part of a larger organisation and to identify strongly with both the organisation and its people. Where the score is high, it will indicate that you have a strong commitment to one organisation; at extremes, it suggests a strong dependency on the current organisation and, in career terms, a total commitment to that organisation to the exclusion of other options.

Altruism

In an increasingly materialistic world, this dimension is often thought to be on the decline. However, it indicates your desire to work for a wider purpose than your own achievement or fulfilment. At high levels, it suggests a really strong motivation to serve others; as a very high score it involves a powerful focus on one particular cause.

Balance

The balance dimension focuses on the extent to which you wish to balance your career with your life outside work. A low score indicates a failure to take other activities into account and to allow work to predominate in your priorities. Higher scores suggest a need to achieve balance between work and the other elements of a full and abundant life. This dimension can change quite dramatically with your current lifestyle – people nearing retirement may exhibit a greater need to develop activities away from the workplace, and people who feel overwhelmed by the volume of work may score higher as a reflection of their need to slow down.

Challenge

Challenge involves the need to set stretching personal goals and to try to find tasks that are difficult and complex, preferably those which have frustrated other people. High scores indicate a competitive nature, not necessarily for the joy of beating someone else but often for the need to set new standards and beat other people's records. High scores in other areas will be a good indicator of the nature of the challenge that you most relish (e.g. high challenge together with high task focus suggest someone who gains real satisfaction from solving difficult managerial problems).

Expertise

Expertise reflects your need to be a specialist or expert in your role. A high score suggests someone who wants to remain within their own profession or specialism for the foreseeable future and is a predictor of their likely career path. People with a high expertise score can be quite happy as managers or entrepreneurs but it is most likely that this will be within their own profession or function.

Financial

Quite simply, this is an indicator of the importance of money in your career. If you have a high score, it is likely that you will see money as an important factor in your career. Taken to excess, financial motivation can often be disappointing as the drive to make money may not be balanced with any of the motivational elements which enable the money to be made and may lead to short-term career development, pursuing the line of best financial return.

Overall

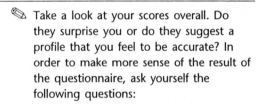 Take a look at your scores overall. Do they surprise you or do they suggest a profile that you feel to be accurate? In order to make more sense of the result of the questionnaire, ask yourself the following questions:

- What are the highest priority work values for you? Is there one dominant value for you? Is there one dominant value or are there two or three with a high priority?
- How are your values reflected in your current role and do they explain any dissatisfaction that you may feel with your current job or your organisation?
- Where have you been most happy and fulfilled? How closely were you connected with your work values?
- Where have you felt least fulfilled and satisfied with your work? Can this be explained by dissonance between your work and your values?

Your motivation to work and your work values are only one facet of your make-up that you need to understand. The next section covers your skills and capabilities.

....

CLARIFYING YOUR PROFESSIONAL SKILLS BASE

Generally there are three key skill areas that you need in order to be fully effective at work:

- technical and professional – the specialist skills you need to acquire in order to be more effective within your own profession
- organisational – the skills of management that all professionals require: marketing, customer service, financial awareness and IT
- personal – the 'enabling' competencies that allow you to make effective use of your technical, professional and organisational competencies; these involve thinking, relating to others and getting things done.

Technical and professional skills are a two-edged sword. When we first start work, the most important development task that we set ourselves is to establish our credibility in our chosen profession. For some people this remains their main career driver, particularly those with a high 'expertise' value on the work value questionnaire. In any profession, there are those who want to deepen their expertise within the profession – lawyers who want to specialise in a particular branch of the law, academics, medical consultants who want to go into research, specialists in industry such as human resource professionals, food technologists and company secretaries.

Your technical and professional skills can be a niche in which you operate very profitably or they can become a 'career cul-de-sac' in which you get trapped and stereotyped. Technical skills are a necessary rather than a sufficient condition for career success – to have a body of professional expertise is a good basis for your career but it is generally not enough to enable you to be fully successful. The specialist in Eastern European commercial law still needs to have the interpersonal skills to influence others and the intellectual flexibility to apply the principles of law to the specific situation.

Many people see their technical background as a springboard to new career opportunities, for example:

- the barrister who moves into business through expertise in commercial litigation
- the pharmacist who moves into pharmaceutical sales
- the fund manager who moves into senior management within an insurance company
- the accountant who moves into general management.

All of these moves depend on factors beyond technical competence – work values, personal competence and the ability to transfer their expertise from one situation to another.

Note down your professional and
technical skills; then identify as many
other fields or professions as you can in
which your skills would be valuable and
transferable.

DEFINING YOUR ORGANISATIONAL SKILLS

The balanced scorecard is a technique that
enables businesses to measure their effectiveness across a range of dimensions to ensure
that they are achieving their strategic objectives. The technique is a useful way of measur-
ing your own effectiveness across the different
organisational / managerial / business skills
required to be effective in today's organisation.

Your personal balanced scorecard will cover
the following four dimensions:

- customer service and marketing
- financial awareness
- IT (information technology) literacy
- people management.

These are the core areas that all professionals
with career aspirations should know, whether
in the public or private sector.

BALANCED SCORECARD CHECKLIST

Measure yourself against this checklist to see if you have these skills in your toolkit.

Customer service

☐ an awareness of the target customer base for your organisation and their main requirements

☐ a good appreciation of the organisation's main products and services

☐ an understanding of the key techniques of marketing

☐ the ability to respond appropriately and with empathy to a customer complaint – even relating to other parts of the organisation

☐ the ability to act as an advocate for your organisation's policies and strategy

Financial awareness

☐ the ability to read and understand the key elements of a set of accounts

☐ an understanding of the processes of financial management and control – budgeting, cost control and forecasting

☐ the ability to interpret financial and statistical information

☐ an awareness of wider macro- and micro-economic realities and their impact on your organisation

☐ an awareness of the financial drivers of your business or sector

IT literacy

☐ the ability to use IT equipment and some basic software – word processing, spreadsheets and presentation aids

☐ an awareness of the possible applications of IT in support of business effectiveness

☐ the ability to use the Internet and the World Wide Web as business tools

People management

☐ awareness of the key elements of progressive human resource (HR) management – the selection, development, management and motivation of people

☐ knowledge of the key elements of employment legislation

☐ understanding of your organisation's human resource policy and procedures

☐ awareness of structures and career paths within your organisation as well as training and development opportunities

☐ understanding of the key activities of other functions and departments within your organisation

---

These are some of the organisational skills that are now required for any manager or senior professional within an organisation. Other important organisational skills are issues such as operating within a legal framework and an understanding of the business planning processes and other key management processes within your business or organisation.

Mark yourself out of 10 for each of the four areas of your balanced scorecard. How will you fill any gaps in your knowledge or awareness?

....

ASSESSING YOUR PERSONAL SKILLS AND QUALITIES

This last section is a chance to review your personal skills and qualities. These are the qualities that enable you to be successful. If the professional and organisational skills are the core of your product offering, the personal qualities are the differentiators, the features that give you your competitive edge and are the real source of your career success.

Many organisations develop competency profiles as the basis for their assessment and performance management processes. These profiles are a useful source of information about the personal qualities that are required by the organisation. Many more businesses are using these profiles for career management and personal development processes so if you can get hold of them, they provide a valuable insight into the requirements of the organisation.

What are your personal skills?

The following questionnaire is intended to provide you with a simple methodology to assess your skills and to get feedback from others. Like the work values questionnaire you did earlier, it consists of a number of paired statements for which you should identify the alternative that you feel you are better at. This is a forced choice questionnaire and so it will give you a sense of the relative levels of ability over a wider set of skills.

✎ The following questionnaire consists of several pairs of statements contrasted with each other. For each question, decide the alternative which you believe to be the more accurate reflection of your skills and abilities and tick the relevant box in the grid on page 31. You may find it difficult to identify the one which is more representative of your capabilities, but try to tick one of the statements. There are no right or wrong answers and nobody else need see what you do. The questions should help you to gain a greater understanding about your core skills and possible limitations.

PERSONAL SKILLS AND QUALITIES QUESTIONNAIRE (PSQ²)

I prefer:
1. A: ☐ Solving complex problems

   B: ☐ Developing new products or services

2. A: ☐ Making high-profile presentations

   B: ☐ Understanding other people's needs

3. A: ☐ Setting goals and objectives for the future

   B: ☐ Applying energy to overcoming difficulties

4. A: ☐ Resolving ambiguous issues

   B: ☐ Making decisions

5. A: ☐ Taking others' views into account

   B: ☐ Choosing between alternatives

6. A: ☐ Understanding the key principles involved in an issue

   B: ☐ Energetically getting things done

7. A: ☐ Identifying innovative solutions to problems

   B: ☐ Persuading people to accept your point of view

8. A: ☐ Taking charge of a situation

   B: ☐ Setting clear priorities for action

9. A: ☐ Speculating about possibilities

   B: ☐ Evaluating different points of view

10. A: ☐ Overcoming resistance to your goals

    B: ☐ Evaluating the risks and rewards of courses of action

11. A: ☐ Seeing trends and patterns in data

    B: ☐ Debating important issues with others

12. A: ☐ Reframing problems to create innovative solutions

    B: ☐ Implementing practical action plans

13. A: ☐ Working out what makes people tick

    B: ☐ Creating efficient systems and processes

14. A: ☐ Ensuring that detailed plans are in place

    B: ☐ Taking an even-handed view of a problem

15. A: ☐ Applying rigorous logic to problems

    B: ☐ Setting clear milestones to enable progress to be monitored

16. A: ☐ Analysing facts and figures

    B: ☐ Being intuitive about people's motives

17. A: ☐ Having sudden insights about a situation

    B: ☐ Bouncing back from problems or failures

18. A: ☐ Generating several alternative ideas

    B: ☐ Supporting and encouraging others

19. A: ☐ Lobbying key opinion formers

    B: ☐ Keeping a cool head in a crisis

20. A: ☐ Creating an influencing strategy

    B: ☐ Cutting through bureaucracy to get things done

21. A: ☐ Providing a service to other people

    B: ☐ Creating a sense of excitement about a project

When you have completed the questionnaire, transfer your responses to the appropriate box in the grid below and count your scores for each dimension, placing the total in the final column.

This is not a psychometric test; it is an indicator of the qualities that you see as your core strengths in relation to your work and career. The questionnaire is deliberately designed to force you to make choices between different statements and so the results may be more skewed than you would expect.

Look at the two or three highest scores and the lowest scores. You may have one particularly strong dimension which will clearly be an important quality for you or perhaps there will be two or three dimensions which when put together will more clearly explain your strengths. Also, there may be one or two dimensions in which you have a particularly low score – this does not mean that you will perform badly in these areas but they will be accepted as relative weaknesses when compared to your other qualities.

Dimension						Dimension Score ↓
Analysis	1A	4A	6A	11A	15A	16A
Creativity	1B	7A	9A	12A	17A	18A
Decision Making	4B	5B	9B	10B	14B	19B
Impact	2A	7B	8A	11B	19A	20A
Empathy	2B	5A	13A	16B	18B	21A
Organisation	3A	8B	12B	13B	14A	15B
Drive	3B	6B	10A	17B	20B	21B

Interpreting your score

The questionnaire is split into three clusters of qualities – thinking, relating and doing. These are broken down as follows:

- thinking is split into three dimensions:
  - analysis
  - creativity
  - decision making

- relating is split into two dimensions:
  - impact
  - empathy

- doing is split into two dimensions:
  - organisation
  - drive.

✎ Work out and write down your cluster score by adding the scores together and dividing by the number of dimensions.

✎ Write down your dimension scores in the grid provided, in order of priority from first (highest score) to seventh (lowest score).

Dimension	Score

You should now have defined the following:

- The cluster of competencies you most prefer – thinking, relating or doing.
- The dimensions you most prefer – analysis, creativity, etc.
- The dimension you most prefer to work in within each dimension – e.g. if you prefer 'relating', do you prefer to work through empathy or impact?

The definitions of each dimension are as follows:

Analysis – the capacity to identify key issues and trends in complex problems.

Creativity – the capacity to look for alternative and unconventional ways to solve intellectual and practical problems.

Decision Making – the ability to look at all circumstances surrounding an issue and decide on a course of action.

Impact – the desire and ability to influence and motivate others to take action.

Empathy – the capacity to work effectively with other people by understanding their needs and motivations.

Organisation – the ability to get things done by effective planning and organising.

Drive – persistence in pursuit of stretching objectives, overcoming difficulties and barriers.

You can give this questionnaire even more validity by asking two or three close colleagues to complete it about you from their perspective. This will give you both valuable feedback and a good impression of the extent to which your own perceptions are shared by other people.

You have now focused on two key issues – your work values and your key strengths. You should have a clear idea of where you are most likely to make your most valuable contribution and where you will gain the most satisfaction at work.

Summarise your capabilities and motivations

✎ Before moving to the next phase of your career review, draw up a matrix to help you summarise the conclusions you have drawn from this section, following the format given in the figure.

High capability; lower motivation	High capability; high motivation
• Area of capability but less satisfaction • Assess whether your strengths in this area are working against your real values	• Area of high promise for career growth • Core strengths, consistent with values
Lower capability; lower motivation	**High motivation; lower capability**
• Area of limited promise for career growth • Area of lower effectiveness, inconsistent with core values	• Area of high motivation but with career growth damaged by lower capability • Focus on development planning to improve skills to match motivation

Capability – motivation matrix

REVIEWING YOUR ACHIEVEMENTS

GOLDEN RULE 2

Look back and learn from your successes and failures.

Before considering more complex and obscure techniques to validate your strengths and weaknesses, you should first look at your past life for clues about your future direction. You have come to the career review with a track record of achievement in a range of different life situations – some commercial, but also some activities which though not work-related are relevant to your working life.

This is all important information for your future career development. This is not to say that the future will be a re-run of the past – it certainly will not. You are, however, likely to be more successful if you are doing things that you enjoy and, by extension, that you do well. The process of self-appraisal involves examining your background and experience to identify where you have a sense of genuine achievement and where you have felt 'in flow' – completely absorbed by the task in hand.

You need to answer the following questions:

- What key abilities or personal qualities have enabled you to reach your current position?
- What are your main achievements at work or elsewhere?
- What do you most enjoy doing?
- Under what circumstances have you been most successful?

What are your key achievements?

✎ Write down the ten things in your life so far that you are most proud of achieving. These may be at work, at home or in your sporting or leisure activities.

✎ Now take the five achievements which
mean the most to you and note down the
following points for each achievement:

• the nature of the achievement
• the important results and outcomes that
were achieved
• the skills and qualities that were utilised
• the work values that were reinforced
• the key learning points – both positive and
negative
• your age or the stage in your personal
development.

....

REVIEWING YOUR FAILURES

Much of the literature about career management and personal development is positive,
and rightly so. As we shall see later, the key
focus for career success is on strengths and
achievements. However, our failures can be
equally illuminating, if slightly more painful
to consider. They tell us about our likely 'no-
go areas' and they tell us about our ability to
bounce back from defeat – there is a saying
that 'failure is not in the falling down but in
the staying down'. Quite possibly, some of
your greatest achievements will have emerged
from your mistakes or failures.

What are your failures?

✎ If it is not too painful for you, write down
a short list of your most dramatic failures.

These can be at work or outside work. Consider things that you did wrong but also things that you didn't do that perhaps you should have. Write a list of up to five and ask yourself the following questions:

- What was the nature of the failure?
- What caused it?
- How might you have prevented it?
- What did you learn from it?
- Was it due to a lack of skill or lack of motivation?
- What was the long-term outcome or consequence?
- What does it tell you about your career and your strengths and weaknesses?

Learn from your mistakes

Remember that there is no shame in getting things wrong. The only way to avoid getting things wrong is to do nothing and that is the worst career strategy of all. People who do more will make more mistakes, but they will also learn more and achieve more in the long term. Reviewing mistakes and learning from them is a more important factor; learning and progressing makes the failure worthwhile and is a much more positive reaction than burying it in your subconscious.

....

YOUR RECENT TRACK RECORD

The next focus is on your most recent employment record. Here, you will review your performance in your current role and the most significant of your previous jobs, assignments or roles.

Your employment record

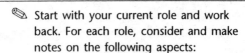 Start with your current role and work back. For each role, consider and make notes on the following aspects:

- your job title and reporting line/s
- the name of the company/organisation/ business unit
- the dates of employment
- your key accountabilities – the five or six key responsibilities that formed the core elements of your role
- your most significant achievements/ contributions – the key things that you achieved while in the role, together with any performance measures available
- the scale of the job – budgets, output figures, sales figures, profitability, numbers of direct reports, etc.
- barriers to success – major problems that you overcame, issues that you faced, difficulties that you couldn't resolve
- key things you learned – how the job developed you and contributed to your personal growth
- what you most/least liked about the job

- why you took the job
- why you left the job
- remuneration – the details of your total package.

Your success factors

You have spent some time evaluating your achievements and your most recent career. You now need to identify the factors that have enabled you to be successful, as these are likely to give you clues about your future levels of job satisfaction and personal success.

✎ For each of the following factors, underline the alternative that most closely fits your preferred approach to work.

- **The level of the role** – did you achieve more in a strategic/planning role, or a more hands-on/operational role?
- **The amount of autonomy** – did you work more effectively as a leader or member of a team, or as an independent operator?
- **The management style of your boss** – did you work more effectively with a more directive boss, or one who gave you wide scope?
- **The nature of the work** – did you enjoy working in a particular area of the business, or were you more involved in a wide view of the business?
- **The level of accountability** – did you manage others, or did you do the work yourself?
- **The nature of accountability** – did you

have prime accountability, or shared?

- **The scope for innovation** – did you develop a new approach to an issue, or were you more effective at putting other people's ideas into operation?
- **The geographical context** – did you enjoy travelling and meeting new people, or did you prefer to work with an established local team?
- **The level of change** – did you enjoy making things happen in a state of change, or do you prefer a more stable environment?
- **The speed of change** – did you prefer dramatic change, or incremental change?
- **The structure of work** – did you work better on one large project, or did you prefer to handle a range of varied issues at the same time?
- **The nature of feedback** – did you work better with regular feedback, or were you content with the occasional 'pat on the back'?
- **The type of reward** – did you need financial incentive, or was the achievement a reward in itself?
- **The status of the job** – did you strive for high status occupations, or were you content to gain the reward for achievement?
- **Learning opportunities** – did you learn new skills, or did you mainly utilise your previous experience?
- **Organisational climate** – did you work better in a stable, structured organisation, or a more informal, fluid business?
- **Networks** – did you develop a wide range of contacts, or did you deal with a relatively small group of colleagues?

- **Location of the activity** – were you dealing mainly externally with customers/clients, or inside your own business?
- **Time management** – were you frantically busy, or did you have time to plan and reflect?
- **Deadlines** – were you under extreme time pressure, or were you given more than enough time to complete the work?

✎ Using the factors in the exercise on the previous pages as thought starters, compile a list of ten factors that have enabled you to function more effectively, within your work or outside of it.

✎ Now compile a list of ten factors which cause you to perform below your best.

....

UNDERSTANDING YOUR NATURAL INTERESTS

Increasingly as I talk to people about their career aspirations, I find it useful to talk about their childhood interests. Often, your interests in childhood or adolescence suggest a powerful motivation or vocation that we often ignore as we move into the world of work. For example, my son has, from a very early stage, been interested in maps and plans – drawing plans of room or house layouts whenever we have had work done on the house. Now this is a useful piece of information as it indicates a real predisposition to planning and mapping; this may lead to a career as an architect, an engineer or an interior designer.

What were the first things that interested you? The things that attracted your attention at an early stage in your life – before you ever thought about your career or thought about earning a living? Sadly, many people find that their early fascinations are ignored in the rush to find a conventional career and the serious business of finding a well-paid job. Later in life, however, when we feel frustrated in our current role, it may be that our true interests are calling us again to resolve some unfinished business. We may not feel like giving up our jobs as an investment fund manager to take up our long cherished aim to be a woodcarver, but we can start to plan our careers to build in more of what we really enjoy doing.

Your interests

✎ Note down your answers to the following questions:

- What were your earliest interests?
- What did you focus on early in your life before you started to think about earning a living?
- What do you do when you have some spare time?
- What is your fantasy job?
- What would you do if you won the Lottery? Would you give up your current role or would you follow some other interest or occupation?
- How would you spend your working day if you had a free choice – indoors/outdoors; working with people or things; organising others or working alone, etc.?

....

SWOT ANALYSIS – AN OVERVIEW

The final part of this section is to start to draw up a SWOT (strengths, weaknesses, opportunities, threats) analysis on yourself. The SWOT analysis is a method used by businesses to understand their capabilities in relation to their markets. In managing your career, you are doing the same – trying to ensure that your capabilities are relevant to the wider marketplace. Identify your strengths and your weaknesses or limitations from your answers to the exercises in this section and draw up the first part of a SWOT analysis, following the format in the figure below.

Strengths	Weaknesses
Your key strengths:	Limitations or weaknesses:
• Your technical base • Your business skills • Your personal skills • Your strongest work values • Your 'motivators' • Your major achievements	• Your weakest work values • Your 'demotivators' • Your areas of least capability • Your major 'cock-up zones'
Opportunities	**Threats**

You will complete the OT element of the SWOT analysis in Part Three of the book.

....

SUMMARY

You must be sure of where you are now before you decide on the best way of moving forward in your career. In this part of *Plan Your Career* you have had the opportunity to look at various aspects of your career and life, which perhaps you have not formally thought about before. In particular, you should now have a good idea of:

- your work values – what motivates you
- your professional and technical skills, and how these could be used in another job or profession
- your effectiveness across different skills areas: customer service and marketing, financial awareness, IT literacy, and people management; and you have thought about how you might rectify any gaps in your knowledge of these areas
- your personal skills and qualities
- your achievements in life and work
- your worst failures in life and work
- your work history, from an analysis of your most recent jobs
- what has enabled you to be successful
- what has motivated you to be successful
- what factors cause you to perform below your best
- your interests, both when you were younger and now.

The self-analysis exercises that you have done have enabled you to complete the strengths and weaknesses quadrants of a SWOT analysis.

Your next task is to think ahead towards the future and the setting of your career goals.

Part two

WHERE DO YOU WANT TO BE?

The SWOT analysis is an important document because it brings together in a coherent way the various factors, internal and external, which have an impact on your future performance and career development. It requires, however, one further piece of work in order to provide you with a good base for a career strategy. The SWOT is only effective when it underpins a set of goals – both for your career and for the other aspects of your life. Your strengths and weaknesses are only relevant when they are compared with the things you want to do in your life.

Clear goals are critical if you are to manage your career effectively. Often we spend our time achieving other people's goals at the expense of our own, and many people end their working life with a feeling of frustration because they have bounced from job to job, taking opportunities as they have arisen without any sense of a clear goal or personal mission behind their career decisions.

This part of *Plan Your Career* takes you through a process of setting goals and is probably the most important part of the career management process. During this process you will do the following things:

- clarify a set of personal goals
- review your current levels of satisfaction with the balance of the key factors in your life and work
- set yourself some specific objectives for the first steps towards achieving your goals.

....

GOALS AND OBJECTIVES

GOLDEN RULE 3

Look ahead and think clearly about where you want to be.

Goal setting is a technique that many people have heard of and not many people carry out. Many business organisations talk about goal setting but prefer to work on objective setting, a key part of the process but not the whole process. In our methodology, goals are broad and aspirational; objectives are specific and measurable. In order to be successful, both factors need to be in place – goals to provide the overarching vision for achievement, objectives to ensure that systematic progress is made towards them. Without goals, businesses and people lose ambition; without objectives, their goals become unattainable because they cannot be broken down into do-able activities. While objective setting is a left-brain, analytical activity, goal setting is an holistic process requiring the use of the full range of faculties, imagination and vision being particularly important.

....

GOALS

Goals are aspirational and identity the broad end results that need to be achieved in a particular activity. There are two sorts of goals:

outcome goals (results focused) and *performance* goals (activity focused). Outcome goals are focused on long-term outcome of activities (winning a gold medal, increasing sales and profit, being the number one in your market, or becoming managing director). They normally involve competing with other people or depend on external factors and not just your own personal competence or motivation. With performance goals, however, you are striving to improve your own performance around areas that you can control.

For example, an outcome goal might be to win the Olympic 5000 metres gold medal, but a performance goal would be to run the 5000 metres in a particular time. Effective goal setting requires a combination of the two – outcome goals are very powerful but need to be supported by some performance goals if they are to be achieved. Athletes know that if they are to win a gold medal, they have to achieve consistently a set of performance goals; they may also require a little more than that on the day of the event, mainly the drive and motivation to exceed their very best performance goals in pursuit of a stretching outcome goal.

I use the acronym **STRETCH** for goals as they should take the individual or business from their current performance and reality and stretch them into a higher level of achievement and activity. STRETCH stands for:

Strategic – taking a long-term, wide view of the activity

Transformational – making a significant change to the status quo

Recorded – written goals are more likely to be achieved

Energising – they should be so exciting that they make you want to work towards them

Trackable – constantly monitored to ensure achievement

Challenging – they should require new levels of capability

Holistic – taking account of the whole of your life or business

Tom Hopkins in his book *The Official Guide to Success* states that goals should be

- believable
- clearly defined
- ardently desired
- vividly imagined
- in writing.

Goals must make you want to stretch yourself to achieve them and they must be the real drivers of your future success – the things that you can't live without doing.

Objectives, however, are the smaller incremental steps that need to be taken if the goals are to be achieved. Big goals without more specific objectives are less likely to be achieved as they remain too big and ambitious to be carried through effectively.

Effective objectives are described as **SMART**:

Specific – clear and unambiguous

Measurable – supported by transparent measures of success

Action-oriented – related to action and not to aspiration

Related – linked to the goals and to each other

Time bound – with a clear deadline

It is true that some people are more clearly goal oriented than others. Some people have clear goals at an early stage in their life; others find that their goals emerge over a period of time. The current and previous holders of the post of Deputy Prime Minister make an interesting comparison: Michael Heseltine is famous for sketching his career on the back of an envelope when at university ('1960s millionaire, 1970s MP, 1980s cabinet minister, 1990s Number 10'), whereas John Prescott claims to have taken each job as it came, from ship's steward to Deputy Prime Minister. One should, of course, be wary of the pronouncements of politicians, but the two make an interesting counterpoint.

The importance of goals

Goals – whether deliberate and planned, or emerging and unconscious – are critical to career success, particularly in the new world of organisational complexity and commercial turbulence. Goals act like a compass in a stormy sea, keeping you on course even during the difficult times. Goals are important for a number of reasons:

- Goals focus your energy on important outcomes rather than dissipating it across a wide range of activities. Focus is as important a word in career management as it is in corporate strategy. People and organisations that have a clear focus, directing their resources and their energies towards a clearly defined goal are more likely to be successful than those who spread their resources and energy too thinly. We all have the same amount of time; it is the way we choose to use it that differentiates us from others. Most time management issues are really issues of focus, how we choose to spend our time.

- Goals give you a template for action. They let you know what your priorities should be at any given time, particularly when linked to an effective form of organisation system.

- Goals focus your attention and enable you to observe things that you have never observed before. In a world that is full of stimuli and information, our brains become adept at filtering out irrelevant data. This is important as it saves us from information overload, but it can prevent us from noticing something important. Once we have a particular goal in mind our brain will actively seek out information that supports that goal and enable us to move forward. If your goal is to become a local politician then your subconscious mind will be tuned in to opportunities to achieve that goal. One of the reasons that successful entrepreneurs identify new business opportunities easily is that their antennae are always out, seeking out new ideas that shoot past other people without recognition.

- Goals provide motivation during the difficult times in your career. If you have a clearly defined goal, you are more likely to overcome barriers than if your goal is vague or ill-defined. If your goal is clearly visualised, it is more likely to remain in vision and so you can continue to move confidently towards it in times of difficulty.

• Other people are more likely to support you if you have a clear goal. Businesses with clear visions of the future are more likely to attract like-minded employees than those that are looking for safety and survival. Likewise, individuals with a clear vision of their own future are more likely to gain the support of their organisation in achieving those goals.

Setting goals

The goal-setting process we will go through can and should be repeated regularly to ensure that goals remain fresh and relevant. They should also be written down – this is critical. Many specialists in the field of personal development refer to a project carried out by Yale University in the 1950s. Conducting a questionnaire among their graduating students, they asked: 'Do you have goals?' Around 10 per cent answered yes. The next question was: 'If so, have you written them down?'. Only 4 per cent answered yes. Twenty years later, they revisited the research group and discovered that those 4 per cent had been more successful than almost the other 96 per cent put together, not just in business but in the full range of other activities in their life.

Writing goals down would seem to have a dramatic effect on the level of the individual's commitment to achieving them and makes the difference between a mission and a dream. I recommend that you write your goals down now and always summarise your reviews in writing. I also recommend that you read and re-read your goal statements regularly. If the goal statement is to be effective it needs to be a life document – the template for your personal plans and the basis for your time management and the guide for setting your everyday priorities.

The next few pages take you through a goal setting process. This should be a very instructive exercise for you and you should emerge from it with a clearer sense of purpose and a better understanding of what you want to achieve in your work and the other parts of your life.

Take time to think about each part of the process. Use the information that you have gathered during the first part of your SWOT analysis to shape some of your thinking, particularly in relation to strengths and 'core competencies', as it is probably from these areas that your goals will emerge.

Be bold in your thinking – think beyond your current reality and your comfort zones. Move towards what you want to achieve, not just what you currently think you can achieve – the act of goal setting unleashes a wave of positive thinking which can overcome some of your current obstacles to success.

Do this work on your own at first. Only share your thinking with other people when you have written it down and clarified it. Some people may feel threatened by your personal goals and put objections in your way (often quite unconsciously) and you need to develop your goals in a positive atmosphere.

Clarifying your goals

What is your mission? Are there important things that you feel you are here in this life to do? Are there certain goals that you want to achieve at work and in the rest of your life? Your career goals must be linked with your other roles in life to be fully effective.

✎ Answer the following questions, bearing in mind the work you did in Part One.

- Where can you make your most significant contribution to your organisation, your family, your community?
- Which groups of people can you support most effectively?
- How would you most like to be remembered?
- What would you most like to do? List five things you would most like to achieve.
- Where do you gain your greatest sense of satisfaction?
- What are your particular talents?

Work/life balance

A further piece of work you may wish to carry out is to identify where you feel that your life and career are in balance and how comfortable you feel with your progress in the different elements of your life and work. This may help you to clarify priorities for goal setting and to help ensure that your work goals are in balance with the other aspects of your life.

| GOLDEN RULE 4 |

Balance your work with the rest of your life.

Many people feel that the issue of work/life balance is one of the most critical facing people at work today. Books such as *Working Ourselves to Death* and *The Addictive Organisation* show that people have real concern about the predominance of their work over the other elements of their lives. It is important to remember that few doctors report people on their deathbeds claiming that they wish they had spent more time at the office. Our work is not fulfilling its purpose if it robs us of the rest of our life; our work goals are only a part of our wider interests and must not become unbalanced.

The Life Balance exercise

✎ Take each of these elements and give yourself a score between 1 and 5 (5 if you feel that everything is working well for you in this area and 1 if you feel that everything is particularly negative). It is unlikely that you will score 1 in any of these areas, but you may give yourself a low mark if you feel that you have some issues to resolve.

Personal growth – your approach to learning and development. This area is critical if you are to grow and develop your career. The greater the challenges in your career, the greater attention you have to pay to your skills. This area includes your recreations and hobbies.

Physical health and fitness – your sense of well-being and your approach to diet and exercise. Health is self-evidently critical to our long-term effectiveness: by definition, dead people cannot be as effective as the living; nor can sick people be as effective as the fully fit.

Mental health and fitness – your motivation, drive and resilience when things go wrong. The world is a difficult and demanding place and you need to cultivate reserves of character for those times when things go wrong as well as motivation and enthusiasm when things go well.

Relationships – your close family and other significant relationships. The most significant gift you can give to your family and friends is your time and this should be a key part of your goal setting and your time planning.

Social – your capacity to get on with people across the social spectrum. Social skills and your responsibilities to your wider community also need to be extended so that this part of your life is enriching and not seen as an afterthought.

Career development – how you feel about your career and your current working life – the theme of this book. Assess how well you feel your career is going now.

Financial – both the reality of your financial condition and your attitude to money. Financial awareness is a particularly important part of good career management. It is high on the list of stresses for many people and yet with good management it can become a positive influence. Building up your net worth is an important goal for your career, as it cushions you against the vagaries of modern life and becomes an important factor in achieving your goals rather than just surviving from one salary cheque to another.

Belief systems – your beliefs, philosophy and ethics. This section is not just a question of religious belief but involves an appreciation of issues beyond your own material welfare. It is a difficult area to assess, but is often the source of strength and recreation in the increasingly turbulent world in which we live and work, giving a sense of perspective to work-based issues.

✎ Make notes on the following:

- What key issues does this exercise highlight for you?
- Where is there scope for improvement and for setting improvement goals?
- What is the overall picture – is it in balance overall?
- What problems currently cause you stress? Is the cause linked to one of these areas?

Balancing your goals is a way of ensuring that your goals are fully integrated with each other. Achieving career goals at the expense of family or social goals is unlikely to produce the satisfaction that you seek, and so the process tries to focus on a range of factors that

underpin individual success. They are, however, just a set of phrases and sentences that
come alive only when they have some activities and measures attached to them.

Identify your life goals

You have answered a number of questions
about the things you want to achieve in your
life. The next stage is to identify the eight or
nine life goals that are high priorities for you.
They are the essential things that must be
achieved if you are to gain fulfilment in your
life and work. These can be split into the
dimensions that you examined in the life
balance exercise earlier in the chapter. These
life goals are the broad aspirations that you
have to achieve in order to be fulfilled across
the range of your life's activities.

Ensure that your goals cover the roles and
activities that you carry out throughout your
life – your role at work, your family responsibilities, your community and recreational
activities. Think about the other factors that
lead to a more fulfilling life – health, personal
well-being, interesting hobbies, and so on.
Check that the key elements of the life balance exercise are part of your goal-setting
work.

One of the most difficult challenges for
setting life goals is that they are often seen as
very broad. Try to find a balance between rigid
and vague goals. The world is changing rap-
idly and people who have very fixed goals are
often frustrated if their target disappears and
they are left without anything to aim for.
Many people have identified a particular job as

their career goal only to find it disappear in a subsequent restructuring of their business.

Equally, a very vague goal is not really a goal at all. Life goals are likely to be quite broad and in some areas may be seen as vague. You should try, however, to focus on specific things that you want to achieve, things that are important to you. As you work through the process, you will become more specific and you will need to move more from outcome goals to performance goals.

You break your life goals down into medium and short-term goals by specifying what you need to achieve over a shorter time frame. I usually suggest ten year goals, three to five year goals, and then annual goals, supported by short-term objectives.

Review and renew your goals every year to ensure that they remain relevant in the light of changing circumstances. As you achieve some of your goals others will become more relevant and you will need to identify new issues; you may also be forced to consider changes in your business environment and develop new goals to overcome these.

✎ Make a list of your life goals, noting for each its rationale.

TURNING YOUR GOALS INTO ACHIEVABLE OBJECTIVES

In order to make the goals come alive, you will need to clarify the key activities attached to them, turn those activities into measurable objectives and build them into your annual, monthly, weekly and daily routines.

The process for carrying this out is as follows.

Break your goals down into activities

For each of your goals, list the main activities that you will need to carry out to ensure that you are making real progress towards your goals. At first, you should work in 'free-fall' to ensure that you are generating as many ideas as possible. Then, go through your list to cut out any ideas that do not support your objectives or which seem impracticable or unlikely (don't be too quick to delete ideas just because they are beyond your comfort zone – we all need some stretch in our lives).

✎ Look at your list of goals and break them down into activities.

'SMARTen' your activities into objectives

We need to turn activities into objectives if they are to be achieved. Personal goals will compete with the day-to-day 'maintenance' activities for our time; we know that important issues are often put to the background compared to more urgent, but often more trivial, matters. At work, our in-tray claims our attention before we go to a meeting of our professional institute to hear about some new approach; at home, we often focus on minor domestic tasks before helping our children with their homework. If we are to focus on more important issues, we have to find ways to manage the delivery of these goals. We can do this by turning them into objectives to be achieved rather than ideals or dreams to be thought about occasionally and then submerged in the mass of daily chores and routines.

Objectives are different from activities because they have a number of additional features. The acronym SMART explains the difference. Ask yourself:

Specific – how clear are my objectives?

Measurable – how will I know when I have achieved them?

Action-oriented – what will they lead me to do?

Related – what goals do they help me achieve?

Time bound – when should I have achieved them by?

✎ Look at your lists of activities and SMARTen them into objectives.

Plan your objectives into your routine

Build work on your objectives into your normal routine. Time management is fundamentally about deciding what is important and focusing on that, while finding ways to deal with the urgent and the routine.

Stephen Covey, the US personal development guru, likens tasks to rocks – important tasks are like large stones, trivial tasks like gravel or sand. If you want to fill a wheelbarrow with stones you place the larger stones first and still have room for the sand and gravel. If, however, you fill the barrow with sand or gravel, you will have little room for the large stones. Likewise, if you fill your life with small tasks, you will leave the large, important issues out; whereas, if you schedule time for the important things – objectives, relationships, self-renewal and so on – you will still be able to deal with some of the trivia.

Plan using the following timescales:

- annual planning – plan your year to ensure that all your objectives for that year are defined and loosely scheduled

- 90-day planning – many organisations are now reviewing their plans on a quarterly basis as annual reviews no longer reflect the accelerating pace of modern business. Take time every quarter to review your plans to identify changing circumstances and new opportunities.

- monthly or weekly planning – a brief review either at the beginning of the month or at the weekend will help to keep your objectives live. With your key objectives, assess each week what progress you have made and how much time you have allocated

- daily planning – every evening, identify six important things you need to do during the next day. Identify the most important and work on it first until it is completed and then turn to number 2, and so on. Focus on the most important when you feel most fresh and energetic,

leaving the routine tasks for times of
relatively low energy.

✎ Prepare an annual, quarterly and weekly
plan for your objectives.

✎ Prepare your first daily plan for tomorrow.

....

BARRIERS TO YOUR GOALS

Many people concentrate on goal setting in
career management and feel that the task is
done. Life has always been complex and
unpredictable and successful people don't just
work on their goals, they have reserves in
place to help them when their goals are not
met. There is a very apt quote from Mary
Pickford, the American actress:

> *'If you have made mistakes ... there is
> always another chance for you ... you may
> have a fresh start any moment you choose,
> for this thing we call "failure" is not the
> falling down, but the staying down.'*

We are judged not by our failures but by our
reaction to failure. It is inevitable that something will affect our career progression and so
we need to have coping mechanisms in place
before problems affect us. There are a number
of ways to cope with barriers to your goals:

- gritting your teeth and keeping going –
  sometimes we believe in the rightness of
  our goal and we ride through the obstacle
- readjusting your goals – stand back and

review the situation and change some of
your short-term goals or objectives
- seeing the obstacle as an opportunity –
  learn from it ... about your reaction to it
  as much as from the obstacle itself
- developing a new goal to adapt to the
  changing circumstances – a better goal
  may have presented itself to you.

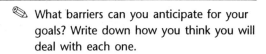 What barriers can you anticipate for your
goals? Write down how you think you will
deal with each one.

....

SUMMARY

In the first part of *Plan Your Career* you looked
at where you currently are in your career. This
part looked at where you want to be. Vague 'I
wishes' and 'if onlys' get you nowhere – you
have to have clear goals and objectives to work
towards. Goals (outcome and performance)
are broad and inspirational; objectives are
specific and measurable. The process of goal
setting requires you to look at both goals and
objectives; reaching your goals requires you to
reach your objectives.

Don't forget to apply STRETCH to all goals
and SMART to all objectives.

You should now have:

- clarified your own goals
- weighed up your work/life balance
- listed your life goals
- broken your goals down into objectives

- anticipated barriers to your goals, and thought of ways of overcoming them.

Now you have ascertained where you want to be, your next task is deciding how to get there.

Part three

HOW WILL YOU GET THERE?

The first two sections have helped you to think about your capabilities and motivation, these factors coupled with your goals and objectives should have helped you to identify your strengths and to create a vision of how you can make them effective in a career. The next phase is to consider a set of generic strategies for managing your career in the short term and the long term.

....

CAREER PATHS

GOLDEN RULE 5

Focus on a career path, not just a job.

There are several elements to career planning, some of which we have already identified. It is rather like a business strategy, involving some planned elements and some opportunistic features. We have already identified some examples of both these types of strategy – you have developed a set of life and career goals and later in this chapter you will, as part of developing your SWOT analysis, identify opportunities in your current role to increase your performance, your personal development and your level of influence.

This section looks forward to the steps you need to take in order to move towards your career goals. These steps may involve several activities – identifying the next job, resolving development needs such as skill/knowledge gaps, or reviewing possible project assignments or secondments to anticipate future changes in the business.

Every business is an internal market with people trying to ensure that their 'products' – skills, knowledge and experience – find the right niche to gain them the best returns in terms of financial reward and heightened influence and reputation. This is good news for the employee in today's business organisation, provided that they are prepared to operate in that market almost as if they were a one person business – 'Me plc'.

There are several broad options for career development within a business, which we will look at now.

Specialise or diversify?

The first issue emerging from an analysis of your core competencies is that of specialisation or diversification. Like businesses, some people have a mission to become a real specialist in a particular area of a profession or industry; others prefer to broaden their skill base dependent on the environment and the needs of their business at the time.

Specialists are able to concentrate their personal and intellectual resources in a particular niche and become pre-eminent. This can be a very powerful position to hold provided that the speciality remains relevant and the specialist is able to keep at the leading edge of their profession. Specialists also need to keep in touch with the needs of their business so that they are not pursuing a professional agenda at the expense of their organisation's goals.

Diversification by learning and developing new skills can also be a fruitful career strategy.

In a time of change, having several options can be useful as organisations re-engineer their processes and, possibly, decide to contract out some of their specialist functions. However, the diversifier must be careful not to end up as a 'jack of all trades' with no professional base of specialist knowledge.

Whichever choice you take, you will need to become either a 'generalised specialist' or a 'generalist with a specialism'. Specialists must see their role in the wider context and generalists must understand their own core competencies and be able to find a niche where they can be put to good use.

Profession or industry specialism?

Another career variable is whether you operate within a professional setting or within a particular industry sector. Specialists can be professionals such as chemical engineers, compensation and benefit executives or criminal lawyers, or they can focus on a particular industry such as food retailing, software development or plastics. Professionals can transfer their skills across industry sectors; industry specialists can move around within their own organisation because they understand the wider picture of the business.

Understanding your particular speciality is important in relation to career development – you need to take career moves which add value to your core competencies, either by deepening your knowledge base or by broadening it. Deepening it makes you more of a specialist; broadening it gives you a wider perspective.

Linear growth or variable?

Career development can take place in two main forms: linear, the career ladder, and variable, the career path. The ladder is a much more direct and simple way to the top. However, if you get to the top of your ladder to find that it is up against the wrong wall, then you are faced with a long way down or the hazardous procedure of moving from one ladder to another.

The career path is a more diverse route to your goals. You may possibly take the occasional detour or wrong turning, but it allows you to maintain your flexibility and may take you to some interesting places that you might not have predicted.

If you are on a career ladder, think carefully about the future – is it the right ladder and will it still be there in the future or will some big rungs be removed? If you are on a career path, ensure that you identify where you want to get to, otherwise you may find that the path takes you away from your intended destination.

Convergent or divergent goals?

Are you aiming at a particular position or role (convergent career path) or do you have a wide range of possible routes to your career goals (divergent path)? Convergent goals are clear and precise but leave the individual exposed if the one job they are aiming at disappears in the next restructuring. Divergent goals lend themselves to flexibility but can be too vague and diverse if they are not clearly defined.

Plot your career type on the matrix set out here and described below.

INDUSTRY

Operators

- Line managers
- Occupation specific
- Focus on increasing contribution and gaining greater accountability
- Organisation or industry career ladder

General managers

- Business unit managers
- Industry specific
- Focus on broadening business horizons
- Career path with promotion and lateral movement

NARROW
FOCUS

BROAD
FOCUS

Specialists

- Professional roles
- Focus on specialised knowledge
- Career growth through deepening expertise
- Professional career ladder

Internal consultants

- Wider specialisms – pulling together the work of different specialists
- Integrating the work of the specialists with the needs of the business
- Career path – moving from specialism to line and back again

FUNCTIONAL/PROFESSIONAL

This matrix is intended to help you think through your broad career path, it is not a template to pigeonhole you or to tie you to a particular box. It describes some broad career types based on two variables – breadth of scope and a focus on either a function/profession or a business or industry.

The **operator** is a role with a focus on a narrow part of a particular business or industry and the career path is likely to remain within that business. Operators often manage quite large areas of the business and have high accountability. Their most likely career move is within their area of expertise, but they can 'break out' into a general management role and their development task is to broaden their expertise and their perspective. Examples are: retail store managers, plant managers, fund managers, nursing managers.

The **specialist** is focused on a narrow part of a profession or function and normally works alone or with a small team. Specialists' most likely career move is to deepen their area of expertise, but they can grow by broadening their scope and becoming an internal consultant. Their development task is to broaden their perspective – either to make a career move or to become a more effective specialist by linking their specialist skills more closely to the needs of the business. Their skills are transferable to other businesses, although they usually stay within the same area of expertise. Examples are: software specialists, compensation and benefits advisers, criminal lawyers, research chemists.

The **internal consultant** normally has expertise in a wider area than the specialist and tends to have a career path that can bridge different businesses and industries, e.g. the human resources director or finance director. They can also move into a general management role by making a decision to remain within one industry or business sector. Examples of 'broad specialists' are in human resources, information technology, marketing, finance and so on.

The **general manager** is normally a generalist but with a focus on a particular sector or business. At the highest level, these people become 'cosmopolitans', people who can transfer their expertise across businesses or sectors for, normally, large salaries because of the breadth of their expertise and their speed of adaptation. Their development is normally a combination of upwards and lateral movements to enable them to gain both accountability and breadth of perspective. Examples are: managing director, business unit director, works manager, senior partner.

✎ Before moving to identifying your ideal career path, ask yourself the following questions:

- In which box do I currently belong?
- Where would I like to be?
- What do I need to do to make the move – broaden my expertise or narrow my focus?
- Where are my real interests – my profession, my business or my industry?
- What are my career drivers – managerial, specialist or some other?
- What are my career goals?

Career planning

This section is helping you develop a plan for your career development by trying to identify the types of career path you need to take to enable you to achieve your career goals. The strategy needs to be developed further by identifying two sorts of issue:

- What sort of experience do you need to achieve your career goals?
- What additional skills do you need?

Broadly, the first issue is resolved by a career plan. The second is resolved by a personal development plan, which is the subject of Part Four.

We have already identified some of the key issues for your career planning – your career goals and your preferred career path. Part of your career development plan will be to agree the sorts of roles that you should be carrying out in the future to enable you to fulfil your potential and to achieve your career aspirations.

Career planning is very different from the mechanistic process it was ten years ago, when, in large multinationals, careers were planned from cradle to grave. Life is no longer a series of promotions but the pace of change at the workplace does require a constant development of skills, knowledge and experience if we are to maintain our effectiveness.

Career planning is now much more individualistic, opportunistic and organic. We expand our skills, our experience and our level of influence in our business continually rather than in a series of rather abrupt step changes. Even if we were to stay in our current job for the rest of our working lives, we would still emerge with a competency profile quite different from the one we have now.

So what are the questions you need to ask yourself if you are to develop an effective career plan? You have already identified career goals, career motivation, the sort of career path that you need to follow and the sorts of role in which you are likely to make your most effective contribution.

✎ Now ask some more focused questions about how you are going to meet those goals and make that contribution.

- What development opportunities are available to you in your present job?

- What additional experience do you need to meet your career goals? Some possible answers here may be:
  - International experience
  - Project management experience
  - Experience of working in another function
  - Experience of working in a different business unit within your organisation
  - Secondment outside the business
  - Membership of a cross-functional working party
  - Exposure to strategic planning
  - Setting up a new function in a recently acquired subsidiary
  - Turning round a struggling part of the business
  - Moving from a central/corporate role to a field role
  - Moving from a field/operational role to a central/corporate role
  - Working with a team reviewing strategy

- What is the next 'step change' move for you? Within the current structure what is the next organisational level and which jobs would be suitable for you at that level?

- How ready are you for that change?

- What opportunities are there for a horizontal move? Expansion can be either upwards or sideways and you may need to acquire experience at your own level to make you a stronger candidate for future roles. Lateral expansion prevents you from getting trapped in a role and can equip you for the future by giving you different experience, allowing you to demonstrate your versatility and endowing you with a new perspective on your business.

- What are your most urgent needs for new experience and perspective?

- What are the next career steps you need to take?

- Whose support do you need to get you there? How will you enlist that support?

....

FINDING A JOB YOU LOVE

I have always found the Greek myth of Sisyphus – who was condemned to Hades where his eternal task was to roll a large stone to the top of a hill and watch it roll down again – to be an excellent metaphor for work in most organisations: people working away for no real reward other than the security of being able to continue to do this work for the rest of their working lives.

Work takes up a large proportion of our lives within most modern economies. Out of our 168-hour week, many people are working and commuting for 50 or 60 hours – half of their total waking time. The pressure and stress involved in these hours seems to be growing and the satisfaction reducing; the recent re-engineering revolution has added to work-loads while reducing security.

What is the response for most people? There are some negative strategies and some positive. The negative strategies first:

- Living for the weekend – this is a relatively simple strategy. It involves putting your life on hold from Monday to Friday, gritting your teeth and climbing on to the 7.40 a.m. train every day, hoping to survive until the first gin and tonic on Friday evening.

- Living for the pension – this is a longer-term strategy. It requires putting your hopes and aspirations on the back burner until you reach pensionable age and can finally start to do the things that you really want to do. The telltale signs of this approach are people who know the rules of their pension scheme backwards and who can tell you exactly how long they have to go to retirement.

- Complaint and subversion – this involves complaining at the coffee machine, trying to win petty victories against the establishment and creating an air of cynicism against the powers that be – focusing energy on resisting rather than supporting the goals of the business.

There are, however, some positive strategies, which can be summed up in the phrase 'Find a job you love'. Spending your most productive years working at a job which is boring and restrictive has to be the worst form of torture. At its best, work creates meaning and adds a new dimension to life; at its worst, it deadens the soul and crushes the spirit. Studs Terkel in his study of American working life saw work as a 'search, too, for daily meaning', but it often became a 'Monday through Friday sort of dying'.

GOLDEN RULE 6

For career success, find a job that you love.

How do you find the meaning without the slow, lingering death?

Change the job

If your job isn't sufficiently challenging, then make it so. Make the job you are doing now into the job that you love. This may be a short-term strategy, but it is important whatever your long-term career choices may be. Your job will consist of a number of components that can be improved or developed in order to make it a great job:

• Can you make a significant improvement in one of the key performance dimensions? Increasing sales, improving service, reducing costs, improving the quality or the timing of a key process?

- Are there new skills that you can learn in your present role that will be helpful in your future career search?

- Are there relationships you can develop – both inside and outside your organisation – that may be both useful and stimulating?

- Can you identify the major stressors in your work and develop a plan to eliminate them?

Change your job

The best long-term strategy if you don't enjoy the job you are doing is to find a job that you do enjoy. I have worked with many clients who create some quite imaginative reasons for staying put – 'the bonus is due in three months', 'my share options mature next year', 'I can take a pension in three years', 'I think we're about to be taken over and I can get a redundancy payment', 'my children are taking their GCSEs/their A levels/cycling proficiency', etc. They are often valid, sensible reasons – often, in life, the most articulate reasons are put forward by people who want to do nothing. The long-term result is that people paint themselves into a corner and when the day comes when they are free to move, the opportunities have gone. Don't rush into another job in a fit of boredom but sit down and identify what sort of job fits your capabilities, values and career goals and then go out and find it. To help you find a new job, read *Job Seeking* by Karen Holmes, another book in the *Career PowerTools* series.

Change your career

A more radical step is to change course completely and to make a career change. This requires more careful thought – but if you find that your current job is less fulfilling than your previous jobs, then it may be that you have made a career choice that may have been right when you made it but is wrong for the person you are now. This requires more careful research – into your own transferable skills and into the entry points and career paths for your new choice.

GOLDEN RULE 7

Look for organisations where your skills can be developed.

It may sometimes mean going back to a career that you enjoyed. I have met several people – headteachers, fund managers, training and development managers – who really want to go back to their original profession because they find the day-to-day grind of management unfulfilling and want to go back to their professional roots. Before a career change, ask yourself the following questions:

- Why am I leaving my current career? What am I leaving behind?

- What other career options do I have? Do they meet my capabilities, my work values, my preferred working style?

- What skills can I transfer to the new career path?

- What preparations do I have to make to transfer effectively? New qualifications? New networks? New ways of working?

- What is the best entry point for the new profession, given my experience and capabilities?

Your job is a temporary phenomenon – a little package of tasks and objectives that have been configured in a particular way for the convenience of your organisation. It is less significant than your long-term career, but it is the current vehicle for your talents and energies and so it is particularly important that you both enjoy it and use it as a platform for your future career growth. Your working life is too short to spend much time in a job that is neither stimulating nor developmental – when that happens, change it or make plans to go somewhere else.

....

FOCUS ON YOUR STRENGTHS

GOLDEN RULE 8

To be successful you must focus on your strengths and manage your weaknesses.

This rule may seem obvious and yet we live in a world that focuses on weaknesses and not on strengths. Go to a parents' evening at any school and the focus will be on the things that your child needs to do better, or on their behavioural problems. Our appraisal processes are geared towards identifying weaknesses and many training programmes are run for reme-dial rather than developmental reasons.

And yet, most of our successes come from capitalising on our strengths rather than avoiding our weaknesses. One of the biggest causes of stress is the view that we should be good at everything – we should be able to think laterally and analytically, we should be good with people and concepts, we should be good with the big picture and the small details.

Many businesses are only just learning that to be truly effective in this complex world, they need to focus on their core competencies, ruthlessly excluding those activities at which they do not excel.

Like the major businesses, we cannot be good at everything. Our task is to identify our strengths and then make them productive, focusing our energies on the areas that will give us the best return. If we can do that we will enjoy a more satisfying career and we will be more productive – our strengths we work on effortlessly because we find them so easy and enjoyable. You don't have to motivate children to do something they are good at, they do it naturally and spontaneously.

There are two key strategies here: identify your strengths and find ways to make them productive, and identify and manage your weaknesses.

Making your strengths productive

You have already done some work on understanding your strengths – what businesses call their 'core competencies'. Where do you truly feel 'in flow', when everything comes naturally and you feel that you master a subject or an activity completely? I recently interviewed someone who felt that they were completely absorbed by the more complex issues of mortgage administration, they had a natural feel for the subject and an interest in it.

How do you make strengths more productive? By:

- identifying your real core strengths and pursuing them actively. Pursue one, not several – you can only sit on one chair at a time. The days of the allrounder are fading in most organisations

- practising your strengths until they become as good as they can be – don't neglect them or take them for granted. Keep your skills up to date and don't assume that because you are naturally good at an activity you will always stay ahead. A recent World Championship Snooker commentator noted that the practice tables were heavily in use during the tournament. To be the best you can be you have to practise

- identifying avenues to use your strengths more productively. Volunteer to act as a coach or to run a training programme; spread good practice in your chosen profession; look for opportunities to make an impact; try to get on working parties and task forces both inside and outside your organisation

- enjoying your strengths and celebrating them. Let people know where your strengths lie and market your expertise as if you were an external consultant to become a respected authority.

How can you make your strengths more productive? Take each strength you identified in Part One, and plan how you will make it work for you.

Managing your weaknesses

Focusing on your strengths doesn't mean that you must ignore your weaknesses. Some weaknesses may reduce your ability to make your strengths fully productive and you need to have some strategies in mind to enable you to manage these. I use the 5D approach to managing weaknesses:

Develop – if a weakness is really standing in the way of your success, you need to develop skills to manage this weakness. It is unlikely to become one of your core strengths, but you may be able to develop it enough to reduce its damaging effects on your performance.

Dump – if something is really dragging you down and causing you problems, then try not doing it for a while. Is that report really necessary? Don't do it for a while and see who squeals. The Pareto principle (the 80:20 rule) tells us that 80 per cent of performance comes from 20 per cent of the effort, and vice versa – dropping those things that don't produce results enables you to spend more time on the things that do.

Divert – find other ways of doing things, divert them to other people (external subcontractors, specialist consultancies and so on). I used to struggle to keep my business accounts up to date until I decided that it was more effective to pay an accountant and free myself from an unpleasant task allowing me more time to do things that I did well.

Delegate – if you have a team of people working for you, select them carefully to mitigate some of your weaknesses. Successful entrepreneurs such as Anita Roddick and Richard Branson bring in effective managers to run the day-to-day businesses, they don't try to do everything themselves. The most compelling reason for not recruiting in your own image is the need to select people who can complement your skills rather than duplicate them. Also, look for complementary partners, people who have skills and approaches that are different from your own and with whom you can form a mutually beneficial partnership.

Drill – if you have a weakness that you can't avoid, set up a mini-process or drill to make sure that you deal with the issue but in the swiftest and least painful way possible. To paraphrase Michael Hammer, the re-engineering guru, 'If you can't obliterate, then try to automate', but do try to obliterate first!

✎ How will you manage your weaknesses? Take each weakness you identified in Part One, and decide how you will manage this in the future.

Focusing on your strengths is productive and satisfying, but mainly it is fun. Doing the things we do best is what most of us want from our work and our lives – it enables us to be really successful rather than just moderately successful.

....

GETTING KNOWN

You have to market yourself effectively if you are to reach your career goals. This doesn't mean indulging in an orgy of self-promotion, but ensuring that your performance is recognised and the people who are in a position to help you fulfil them know your career aspirations. You must continue to focus your energies on your business performance and personal development to ensure that your 'product' is of high quality. However, you must ensure that your achievements are visible and that you have a strategy that differentiates you from others so that you are not 'just another accountant' or a 'typical HR person'.

Many British people regard self-promotion as an embarrassing trait and people who promote themselves are seen as 'blowing their own trumpet', which is really 'not done' in our culture. Self-promotion is not a sin or a personality defect, it is a way of making people aware of what you have done and what you want to achieve.

| GOLDEN RULE 9 |

Get out more and expand your network.

You need to ensure that you promote yourself positively at all times. Whatever you do, you leave an impression – positive, negative or neutral. You need to ensure that the impact you have is positive rather than negative or neutral. Personality comes from the Greek word *persona*, the mask worn by actors in Greek drama. You need to ensure that the mask you wear at work highlights your most positive features by:

- using optimistic and positive words and phrases
- acknowledging your achievements and accepting praise without embarrassment
- focusing on what you can contribute to any situation or project, not on what you can't contribute
- acknowledging other people's contribution and giving credit
- selling ideas and concepts to work associates with enthusiasm not diffidence
- creating a sense of momentum and energy
- embracing, rather than resisting, change.

Networking

Rosabeth Moss Kanter in *When Giants Learn to Dance* identified two key elements in job security and employability: the skills you possess and the people you know. Your network of contacts is critical to your growth and success, not just as sources of work but as sources of inspiration and support. A key marketing activity will be the creation and development of a network of contacts that can support you in your career objectives and your personal development. We look at this briefly here, but for more detail, please refer to *Powerful Networking* by the same author and also part of the *Career PowerTools* series.

Some people see networking as a process of

exchanging business cards with people in the hope that one day they will be able to 'do them a favour' or provide other business contacts. It is a more subtle and comprehensive process than that, each contact providing a different perspective from yours and, possibly, identifying different opportunities for your development. Some people provide you with ideas, some with support, others may give you access to other contacts; some may just be people you like working with and who make you feel good about yourself.

✎ There are several categories of contact; identify two or three examples of each during the next section.

Categories of contacts

Gatekeepers – people who have a wide variety of contacts and who can give you access to other people or other organisations. Within your organisation, it may be your HR manager or your line manager.

Mentors – people who will give you advice, support and feedback. Mentors need not always be senior line managers or people within your own organisation. Who do you turn to for advice and who is sufficiently objective and sensitive to give it to you in the right way?

Soul mates – people whose company you enjoy and who give you support and encouragement. Life in the modern business organisation is tough and you need people to talk to and relax with if you are to retain your sanity and your commitment to your goals.

Role models – people who have done what you are thinking of doing and may be prepared to give you advice and guidance. The best person to tell you about climbing Everest is the person who has just been photographed with the flag on the summit. Beware, however – they are different from you, with different skills and style, and so use them to find out what it's like, not how to do it. Use their experience as a guide not a template.

Authority figures – people with authority and seniority that have the clout to make things happen for you and to introduce you to a network at a higher level. Like all powerful people, these can be dangerous – they may develop their own perspective on what your goals should be and not what you want them to be. However, top people can be useful and open the doors to the corridors of power that would otherwise be closed to you.

Coaches – bosses from whom you can learn specific skills and who are enthusiastic delegators. If you work for one, use the time wisely, as there are few of them around! If you happen across one – perhaps someone leading a project team that you work on – be sure to identify the skills you can learn from them and develop an explicit development contract with them. They will be far more committed to coaching you if they understand your needs and the key things they can support you with.

Complementary partners – an increasingly common business strategy is the development of core competencies and the formation of alliances with other organisations possessing complementary skills to create a new product or service. This is a useful career strategy, too – find people with sets of technical and personal skills different from yours and work together to develop a new service for your business. For example, the human resources director could work together with the finance director to create a financial awareness package to support a cost management programme.

Protégés – look to support people who are on their way up in your business. They are often the people with new ideas and fresh perspectives. Spending time with them will stimulate your own thinking as well as gaining you a reputation for being a good person to work with and a good coach.

The different types of contact may not always come from your own organisation. They may be colleagues, friends, former colleagues, family, members of the same professional institute, people you meet at conferences, social contacts, community leaders, members of local business organisations and people you meet on holiday. The list of potential contacts is endless and so the following guidelines may help you to form and grow your network.

Guidelines for networking

- Be prepared to talk about your goals and objectives to identify points of mutual interest with contacts.
- Keep records of names and addresses as well as personal notes on background,

family and interests – a simple card index will be enough.

- Reciprocate – don't just think what your contacts can do for you, think what you can do for them.
- Learn to develop rapport with people and move from formal to informal discussions as soon as possible – greater intimacy generally leads to more productive outcomes.
- Initiate contact with people in as many situations as possible – you may meet valuable contacts in the boardroom or outside your children's school.

People to avoid

As well as people you should seek out, there are some people you should avoid:

- stress carriers – people who drain you of energy and optimism
- cynics – people who tell you that a thing can't be done when what they mean is that they couldn't do it!
- competitors – people who may have very similar aspirations and who might block your own plans in order to further their own ambitions.

Virtual network

One further network you should develop is your virtual network – a group of figures who you can consult on an imaginary basis. Appoint a fantasy board of directors to give you advice and support and consult them in your reflective times; you have carte blanche to appoint anyone you wish. If you need to create a vision for your team, consult John Harvey-Jones; if you are taking some risks, what would Richard Branson advise, or Napoleon, or Julius Caesar? Who are your heroes and heroines, what have you learned from their lives and what would they say to you about your own challenges?

....

CHANGING CAREERS

| GOLDEN RULE 10 |

Know when to make a career change.

Charles Handy has noted the S-curve theory of change in his books *The Empty Raincoat* and *In Search of Meaning*. He describes it as the way of all change – starting slowly, picking up speed, peaking and declining. At one time, we went through one curve in our lives; now, we live through several in our lives and our careers.

One exercise that career counsellors do is the timeline – getting people to look back on their career and review its significant moments in a linear progression. In a complex world the linear progression is no longer as relevant as the series of S-curves, the reality of our career is not a long line of unbroken progression from induction to retirement. We make moves, we grow and develop in a role and then we either peak and decline or we move into a new role and start at the bottom of a new learning curve. The S-curve is an important factor in managing your career – it is part of the secret of maintaining momentum and keeping the pace of development going.

There are three important tasks implicit in the S-curve pattern:

- managing your current curve as effectively as possible – managing the present
- looking towards your next S-curve and predicting what it might be – envisioning the future
- managing the transition from one curve to another – managing the change.

Managing the present

Much of the literature of career management is filled with advice about the future. But whatever you do in terms of goal setting as you read this book, you will still need to go into work tomorrow or next week in, probably, the same job you are doing today.

You will still be on your current S-curve, working on some of the same issues. However, you can start to work on them with a different perspective and working towards clearer goals – identifying ways to increase your contribution, to develop new skills and to gain a greater influence on the ways things are done. Managing the present is an important part of your future career management but it is not the only part.

Envisioning the future

The most difficult issue in career management is envisioning your S-curve of the future – the next major stage in your career and what it will look like. The philosopher Kierkegaard said wisely that life is understood backwards but has to be lived forwards, and for many of us it is easier to look back and see previous career changes and to understand their logic in hindsight but the future is more difficult to see. Scenario planning can help you cope with uncertainty in the future and we look at this later in this section.

Allow yourself some time to think about your future curve. Build future planning into your schedules and plans. The lesson from organisations is that businesses that concentrate only on the present often don't have a future; nor, of course do businesses that only think about the future to the exclusion of the present day. You need to develop a bi-focal ability and learn to adjust your vision from close to long distance vision and back again.

Managing the change

One of the most critical decisions for any organisation or individual is when to move from the present curve to starting a future curve. The simple answer proposed by Charles Handy is to start a new curve before the existing one reaches its peak so that you make the move when things are going well. The change then becomes a fluid movement from one state to another and not a jerky, scrambled leap in despair from a sinking ship to a lifeboat.

Many people who are made redundant move into another difficult business situation because in their haste to find a new job they leap into the first opportunity that arises. They had not given any thought to what their second curve might be until a change was forced upon them and so they are unprepared for a major change, particularly if they had felt themselves to be at the peak of their career with their existing organisation.

We must always be asking 'What next?', even when the status quo is so apparently positive.

How do you know when to change?

You should always have a second curve in mind, even when you are just starting up your first curve – the further up the first curve you go the more urgent the clarification of the next curve becomes. There are signs that will indicate when you are nearing the point to make more significant changes in your career:

- the sense that you have been round a particular loop before – that the work you are doing is becoming routine and teaching you nothing new. (This is not the same as remaining in the same job. If your job keeps presenting you with new challenges and you remain stimulated by it, then stay with it)

- the sector you are in is in decline or stagnant and there are no new ideas or opportunities for growth

- your own feelings of frustration or stagnation. The 8 o'clock on a Sunday evening test – do you look forward with anticipation to Monday morning, or to next Friday evening?

- the feeling that you are completely on top of your job and totally in control; this is a sign that you are near the top of your first curve and the only way is down. A certain amount of discomfort is no bad thing in that it forces you to establish new ways of working and to think about new ideas. Being too comfortable is more dangerous than being uncomfortable – it leads to complacency.

....

COMFORT ZONES

Breaking out of your comfort zones is one of the most important principles for life-long career management. Progress is only made by breaking out of what we know and heading towards what we don't know. In all spheres of human endeavour, people make real strides only by tackling things that they find difficult. We do not get better at tennis by playing people who are worse than we are; we get better by taking on better players and finding new levels of performance from within ourselves. Businesses don't get better during periods of trade protection, they grow when they are exposed to a competitive market, however painful that may sometimes be.

GOLDEN RULE 11

To make progress, break out of your comfort zones.

Stretching beyond our comfort zones is important because it forces us to find new reserves and resources deep inside ourselves. It is also important because by creating our own pressure we learn how to manage stress in a controlled way so that when an external pressure is put on us, our coping mechanisms are in place and we are ready to rise to the new challenge. When we have no tested coping mechanisms, any external stress overwhelms us, and so breaking free of our comfort zones enables us to develop those mechanisms in a controlled way before they need to be tested in combat conditions.

Managed change is an important strategy for career management. Making changes in your career in your own time before they are forced upon you by circumstances allows you to be in charge of your own career, not the victim of organisational restructuring or changes in the business cycle. Identifying what your future should be like, understanding how to get there and knowing when to make the change has to be a more attractive long-term strategy than sitting tight in your corporate bunker and awaiting events, however comfortable that bunker might be.

Avoiding danger is no safer in the long run than outright exposure. The fearful are caught as often as the bold.

(Helen Keller)

....

THE OT PART OF SWOT

The first place to start in the management of your career is your current role in your current business. The second part of the SWOT analysis you began in Part One involves identifying opportunities and threats. To do this effectively you will need to examine your organisation in a way that you may not have done before. Adopt the mindset of the entrepreneur, constantly looking for opportunities to do new things, to increase your visibility and to enhance your contribution.

In the following sections, you will go through a systematic review of opportunities and threats within your current organisation. You will look at three types of opportunity:

- opportunities to increase your contribution to the business results
- opportunities for career development and to learn new skills
- opportunities to gain greater influence in decision making.

GOLDEN RULE 12

Be alert for opportunities within your current role.

Opportunities to increase contribution

Expanding your contribution in your current role is an important career strategy. Excellent performance in your current role enables you to become more visible without apparent self-promotion and provides you with a track record which can form the basis of your future career growth. Any career strategy not based on good performance will eventually fall away through lack of substance.

Many organisations have conducted extensive delayering exercises and this has increased the size of jobs and the space between one job and the next higher level. This has increased the scope for expansion within the job rather than growing through moving between jobs. The delayered organisation requires people who, using their own initiative, see the job description as the core of the job, a base for further exploration rather than the job itself. The effective manager for the future will be managing the 'white space' in the job rather than the written structure. The white space can be found in the goals and strategies, both actual and emerging, of the business or organisation. A good knowledge of the long-term aims of the business and the environment in which it operates gives them an important edge in knowing where to direct their efforts.

About your organisation

✎ Identify and clarify the following questions about your organisation:

- What are the key goals of the organisation?
- What are the goals of your division or department?
- What are the likely future changes in your business or industry?
- What is the impact on your business of current economic, political, social, technological and demographic changes?
- What changes in your profession or specialism can be used within your organisation?
- What are the 'core competencies' of your business?
- What noticeable weaknesses hold your organisation back?

- What features of other businesses (competitive or non-competitive) can be used within your own business?
- What unmet needs are apparent to you within your organisation?

About your job

Examine your job to identify where you have the scope to increase your contribution and therefore increase your value to the business. Typically, job descriptions have the following features:

- purpose – a one liner (usually) clarifying the contribution that the jobholder should be making to the business
- accountabilities – a set of critical success factors which if met successfully lead to a fully effective performance
- measures – a group of measures that enable the jobholder to monitor their own performance
- competencies – a set of technical skills and personal qualities that enable the jobholder to perform effectively.

Each of these features offers opportunities either to increase your contribution or to develop new skills.

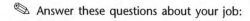 Answer these questions about your job:

- How can you achieve the job purpose more effectively?
- What scope is there to add to the job's key accountabilities?

- Which of the accountabilities can be carried out more effectively?
- Which of the performance measures can be increased significantly?
- Where could you make the biggest impact in terms of improved business performance?
- Which areas take up significant effort for little return? Can these be made more efficient or stopped altogether?
- Are there areas where you need more technical skills?
- Are there additional personal competencies that would improve your current performance?
- Where is there scope for continuous improvement and where is there scope for radical change and innovation?
- Who are your main 'stakeholders'? What unfulfilled needs do they have? How can you support them more effectively?
- What opportunities exist for you to leverage your own specialist/technical knowledge?

Opportunities for career development

This section requires some systematic thinking about the opportunities for career development.

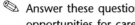 Answer these questions about your opportunities for career development:

- What are the skills and competencies most valued by the business?

- What skills and competencies will be required for the future?
- What are the pivotal (i.e. the key operational or strategic) jobs within the business?
- What are the career development mechanisms within your organisation?
- Where are the emerging 'new business' projects?
- What competencies do you require to carry out your present job effectively?
- What new skills are becoming more important within the business? What do you need to do to develop them?
- What new projects are being developed? How can you become involved with them?
- What career path are you following? Do you see yourself as a general manager, a 'functional' specialist or a 'business' specialist?
- What opportunities exist for promotion to a higher level?
- What opportunities exist for a horizontal move to another part of the business?
- What do you need to do to capitalise on these opportunities? What would they add to your skills and employability?
- What training and development opportunities exist? Which ones support your developmental objectives?
- What are the core business development programmes? How can you get on them?

| GOLDEN RULE 13 |

Seek more influence on critical decisions.

Opportunities to gain greater influence

The third area for identifying opportunities within the business is that of gaining greater influence. This area is based on success in the two previous areas – influence is a factor of increasing performance and personal growth but it requires other skills as well. There are some good performers who gain little reward for their efforts because the people who are able to promote their careers do not see enough of them. They feel that self-promotion is unworthy and so they toil away, becoming increasingly embittered about their lack of visibility and career progression.

Promotion without performance is undoubtedly 'hype' and of little value. However, performance needs promotion if it is to reach a wider audience. Even the best products need advertising if they are to achieve market share and part of your career strategy will be to market yourself more effectively.

✎ Consider the following questions:

- Who are the people with real influence in the business? How well do you know them? What do they think of you?
- What opportunities do you have to increase your visibility?
- If you were a 'brand', what image would you project?
- How would you define the organisation's style and culture? How does that fit with your own?
- Where can you link together people or ideas that are currently disconnected?

- What external networks do you belong to and how can you import ideas and connections from them into your organisation?

Threats

Most of our work focuses on opportunities but, in a changing and complex working environment, it is important to have an awareness of the potential barriers to career development or growing one's personal contribution. Some questions may help to identify these and this will enable contingency plans to be developed for the future.

✎ Answer these questions relating to potential threats:

- What are the key changes taking place in your organisation?
- Will these have a positive or negative impact on your development?
- What might the negative consequences be? How can you prevent or minimise their impact on your position?
- What are the key changes taking place in your industry (such as new entrants, changes in legislation or technology, globalisation and changes in consumer behaviour)?
- What can you do to help your business adapt to them?
- What impact will these changes have on your current role or future progression?
- What internal threats do you perceive within

the business? What are the forces that might prevent you from achieving your career goals?

- What kind of scenarios do you envisage for your career? What could happen – as best case, worst case or most likely case? What plans do you have for each of these scenarios? How resilient are your career plans?
- Are there any difficult relationships within the business that might create barriers to your career development?

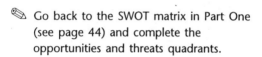 Go back to the SWOT matrix in Part One (see page 44) and complete the opportunities and threats quadrants.

....

PREPARING FOR UNCERTAINTY

GOLDEN RULE 14

Plan ahead – prepare for an uncertain future.

One factor which makes effective career management difficult is the unpredictability of the modern world. The speed of social, economic and technological change is so great that it makes it very difficult to make plans on the basis of sound information. For many people this uncertainty has come as a shock, particularly the generation that started work in the 1950s and 1960s when there was a much higher degree of stability and the decision to join one of the large corporations, such as Shell, BP, ICI, Barclays Bank or GEC, was almost certainly for life. Many of the casualties of downsizing in the last few years were often shell-shocked because they had no expectation of having to look for another job.

The experience of the last few years means that employees are now much more aware of the likelihood of some form of change in their working lives. However, few people are building this uncertainty into their career plans, preferring to bet on one 'preferred future' rather than have a range of options in place.

One technique that businesses use to plan for the future in an uncertain world is 'scenario planning' – a technique borrowed from the military strategists by Royal/Dutch Shell to help them develop more robust business plans. The technique came to prominence because Shell, unlike the other oil companies, had put plans in place to anticipate the increase in oil prices during the 1970s and so was better prepared to change to meet the new environment. The point about scenario planning is not to be exactly right about the future but to start to think of a range of possible futures and prepare for them. The dangerous alternative is to plan on the basis that the future will be an extension of the past and extrapolate accordingly.

The relevance for individuals is that the future is, as always, unpredictable, and yet many people have no real sense of the possible scenarios that may arise. What are the likely changes in your business within the next five years? What will your industry sector look like within ten years? How will your profession have changed within the next fifteen years? If you are thirty now, then these questions take you to age forty-five! Think back to the changes in your career to date – then assume that a faster rate of change will take place in the next twenty years. What possible futures can you see then?

How do you start to anticipate the changes? The following is a very brief methodology to help you anticipate the likely changes in your own organisation.

Step one – define your issue

This may be as simple as 'Should I change my career/job in the next few years?' or 'What will happen to my business/industry/sector?' It may deal with a specific issue, such as 'Should I move into management or stay in a more specialised job?' or 'Should I consider becoming a self-employed consultant?'

Step two – clarify the key factors which may affect your decision

This involves listing the types of factor that, within your immediate environment, may be relevant – changes in customers, suppliers, competitors etc. It may involve thinking beyond your sector into the wider environment – the state of the economy, the impact of emerging technology, demographic trends, legislation, ecological issues and so on. The nature of the factors will depend on business and your question. You may be asking a very broad question – what new business sectors may arise during the next few years? – in which case your enquiries will need to be very broad; other questions may require a much more narrow field of enquiry.

Step three – research the key factors

Read widely and talk to as many people as possible within your business, profession and industry. Look at journals you wouldn't normally read about issues that you might not usually consider. Orion's series, *Predictions* may help you think through a particular topic such as population, climate, warfare, the media and so on. *The Economist* is a good source of information about future trends as are *Fortune*, *New Scientist* and a range of weekly journals. Talk to people within your own business about their perception of the future and then discuss your findings with them if you can. It is important, however, to look for trends and not fads.

GOLDEN RULE 15

Ride trends, not fads.

Trends are significant changes in social, economic, technological or political realities whereas fads are transient phenomena that become popular quickly and fade with equal speed. The ageing population is a trend, indisputable in its reality and its impact; some of the other phenomena which flit across the nation's boardrooms are less critical, although, like stock market speculation, some people can make short-term profits from these fads.

Step four – identify some possible scenarios

Draft out three scenarios with different outcomes. Unless there are particular issues you want to address, you may wish to develop three different scenarios – industry growth, retrenchment, and 'more of the same' – an extension of the status quo. The growth scenario is an important one – many of us are so used to retrenchment that growth takes us by surprise. We miss opportunities if we don't prepare for growth and periods of growth are the times when we are most likely to find ways of developing our career and learning new skills.

Step five – understand the implications of each scenario for your career

Identify for each scenario the main implications for your career – what kind of roles would you target, what new skills would you require and what new possibilities would each scenario offer to you? Some of these you may feel are irrelevant but some may give you an important insight into a new career opportunity. Remember, the scenarios will not always come true but they will provoke you to find out more and think more about the future and the sorts of skills and development opportunities you will need to follow.

Step six – identify pointers and indicators for the future

You will need to identify some indicators that will help you to know which of your scenarios is becoming a reality. You will also need to keep this process going, watching important trends closely so that they don't take you by surprise. The whole point of scenario planning is to develop greater flexibility and to think more closely and systematically about the future.

Scenario planning is an important way to keep alert and confident about the future. Like Shell during the oil crisis, you will be able to anticipate events because you will be prepared to accept change rather than go through the usual process of denial and reaction.

....

SELF-MARKETING

Whether we like it or not, people, like products, develop or acquire a 'brand image'. When we think about our colleagues at work, certain words or phrases come to mind – 'solid and dependable', 'someone who gets things done', 'a high flier', 'a marketing specialist', 'a problem solver' and so on. This is what advertising agencies do when they advertise a product, they try to create an image or concept that sets the product apart from its competitors. The brand image differentiates the product from the commodity.

GOLDEN RULE 16

To be successful you must be your own marketing consultant.

You have to market yourself effectively if you are to reach your career goals. As we have already said, this does not mean indulging in an orgy of self-promotion, but rather ensuring that your performance is recognised and your career aspirations are known to the people who are in a position to help you fulfil them. The product has to be good if it is to be marketed effectively, otherwise the adverts are just empty hype (remember the 'Listening Bank' that didn't listen!). Likewise, you must focus your energies on your business performance and personal development to ensure that your 'product' is of high quality, but you must also ensure that your achievements are visible and that you have a strategy that differentiates you from others.

Marketing yourself as 'Me plc' requires the classic marketing 4 Ps but defined slightly differently – people, product, promotion and perception. People has already been covered in the Networking section (see page 91) but the other Ps are set out below with guidance on how to manage them.

Product

It has been said that 'everyone lives by selling something'. You have already done a lot of thinking about yourself – your strengths and weaknesses; your core competencies and contributions; your values and style. Now think of yourself as a product.

Answer the following questions about your 'product':

- What are the key features of your product? What are you able to sell to your business and the world outside? What are your key features – your specialised knowledge, your ability to thrive in certain situations, your management skills, your personal qualities?

- Who are your customers? Who benefits from your product or service currently? Who might benefit in the future? What additional needs do they have?

- What differentiates you from others? People can never be a commodity. We all have unique characteristics and experience which enables us to make a different contribution to our business. What makes you unique? What blend of skills, experience and approach makes you different from your colleagues?

Promotion

How will you go about promoting your product without overselling or embarrassing yourself and others? We have already noted that self-promotion is a difficult thing to do for many people and you will need to do this very subtly. The first person you need to convince is yourself. Read back through the notes you made in Part One and focus for a while on your achievements. Examine your successes and identify the things that you did to achieve them. Those skills, competencies, behaviours and attributes are permanent features of your product offering, which can be transferred to other situations and contexts. These should give you the confidence to promote yourself actively and seek out new challenges, confident that you can bring those same talents to bear in different circumstances.

How do you begin to promote and market yourself? Self-marketing is the application of the basic principles of marketing but applied to a unique product – you!

- Identify your target markets, customers and stakeholders and then ensure that you understand their needs and promote yourself actively to them.
- Understand your unique selling proposition (USP) and develop and build on it.
- Build credibility by delivering quality services and doing excellent work.
- Ensure that the people who should know about you and your work do know about it – make presentations, write articles and take a leadership role in external or internal activities.
- Benchmark your performance against other people – identify excellent people within your field and try to understand what makes them effective. Don't imitate them, but try to build some of their strengths into your product offering.

✎ Make notes on how you could promote yourself.

Perception

We often talk about reality and how things are in the real world. In managing your career effectively, you must give thought to how things are perceived. Perception is reality, everything we see and do is filtered through our senses and our feelings and so what we regard as reality is really our *perception* of reality. Hence, you need to pay attention to how you are perceived – what is the brand identity of your product? In order to understand this, you will need to get freedback from your colleagues about their perceptions of you.

- What are your strengths and weaknesses?
- Where do you add value to their work and where do you detract from it?
- What are your most positive characteristics and what are the things that you do that get in the way of your working relationship with them?
- What words would they use to describe you?

A simple way to get this information is to ask people directly; sometimes, you may prefer to ask indirectly by getting feedback on the projects that you have worked on for them or asking them a more general question about your team. Ask your boss at your appraisal interview and create an environment within your team whereby feedback is exchanged openly and freely. Your organisation may have a 360° feedback process in place and you will gain much useful information from this sort of activity.

Marketing yourself is not the only factor in career success but lack of a personal marketing 'plan' will surely lead to derailment at some stage in your career as others' perceptions of you become increasingly important as you progress within your current organisation or you move elsewhere.

....

THE BIG PICTURE

The one factor that differentiates high fliers in a business from their management colleagues is the size and scope of their thinking. It is not necessarily their intellectual power that counts but the way they apply it. Some people bring a powerful intellect to bear on relatively unimportant problems, the real high flier looks beyond the smaller problems and focuses on the big picture, the wider implications of their work.

GOLDEN RULE 17

Always look at the big picture.

Looking at the big picture can be done in a number of ways.

Be ambitious for yourself and your work. Don't set goals which are easy to achieve, try to set demanding and expansive goals for yourself and others. Many management trainers emphasise the need to make goals and objectives achievable and so that's what many managers do – they set themselves achievable goals and then wonder why they are so bored at work! Successful people set themselves bold and audacious goals because that forces them to draw on new reserves of courage and innovation as well as making their working life more interesting. In your projects and activities look beyond the safe, secure, achievable objectives and try to find ways to astound your colleagues, to get them to say 'How did they do that?'

Think beyond the familiar routines of your work to try to understand how your job impacts on the wider business strategy and how it might be done more effectively. Even if your role isn't 'strategic', you can demonstrate your understanding of the big picture by relating it to the organisation's wider purpose and looking for ways to increase your contribution and the contribution of your team. Take every opportunity you can to talk to decision makers and influencers within the business to understand their perspectives and to demonstrate the breadth of your own thinking.

Express yourself with confidence at all times – people will take you at your face value and if you devalue your achievements and the achievements of your team then so will they. Use bold and strong words, don't discount yourself by using little, self-deprecating expressions – we are on a marketing campaign at work and the way we describe our product is the way people will perceive it. After a while, even if you are not particularly confident, the positive words and phrases that you use will start to have an impact on your own self-confidence and will programme your mind to think positively about your work.

Always approach each task with a clear

vision of what you want to achieve and get others to feel committed to this vision. Don't start a project by plunging into the details but spend some time looking at its wider implications and the needs of the project's stakeholders before trying to create a vision that exceeds expectations rather than merely meets them. You will find that a clear vision of what can be achieved will act as a powerful motivator to get some of the detailed work done as your colleagues will have an exciting view of the end product in mind rather than a dull and conventional picture.

Take the high ground on issues and think through the larger implications. Avoid pettiness at work and negativity, prefer to be seen as someone who focuses on the 'critical few' issues rather than the 'trivial many'. For example, try not to become obsessed with cutting costs in your section but look to see how you can add the most value; don't get involved with political games or turf wars, prefer to highlight how the organisation can meet its goals and improve its competitive positioning.

Develop a wider awareness of the world around you. Deliberately study new subjects and read widely about factors beyond your own organisation or your own industry. Set out to broaden your horizons and experience by reading new books or journals, watching new films and visiting other organisations in different sectors.

Mix with talented and imaginative people. One of your goals in your networking campaign should be to meet people who have ideas different from yours and who can expand your horizons. I know of many people who only network with people like themselves

– all they succeed in doing is reinforcing their own prejudices.

....

SIMPLICITY

We have already touched on the importance of focus in effective career management. Focusing on strengths and on the activities that are most likely to bring the best rewards. This is often easier to prescribe in principle than it is to carry out in practice. At both work and home, we are under pressure to do and be everything. We have so many claims on our time as professionals, managers, parents and people that trying to maintain our focus on the really important things is becoming increasingly difficult.

Recently, many books have appeared, mainly in the USA, on the topics of downshifting and simplicity. Downshifting is the philosophy of opting out of the rat race for a simpler and less stressful way of life. I am not advocating that you immediately head off to the Orkneys to set up a pig farm or that you go to the Bahamas to run a bar – attractive as those two options might seem. I do believe that the downshifting trend is important and has some messages for the wider management of your career. The importance of simplicity and of not trying to do it all, focusing on the really important issues – your career goals, your key accountabilities, your family, your health and so on.

Simplifying your life enables you to keep your energy focused and helps you manage stress more effectively. Setting yourself stretching goals is stressful enough without having to deal with a wide range of trivia. Time management systems, electronic mail and personal organisers have helped people manage their time more effectively but may have added to the complexity of their lives by giving people the technology to deal with an ever increasing range of activities. Each item of new technology brings potential for time saving but it is also an additional item to maintain and carry around. If a simple diary and notebook system works for you, don't invest in an electronic organiser. Obliterate before you automate – remove activities before you look at working more efficiently.

GOLDEN RULE 18

Keep things simple.

Tips for simplicity

Focus your time and energy on the things that give the best return in the long term – building relationships, working on new ways of doing business, personal development for yourself and your team, developing an effective network and your key accountabilities. Spend time developing the future rather than just fixing the present. Remember the 80/20 rule – 20 per cent of the effort leads to 80 per cent of the results. Try to identify the specific efforts that lead to the results and spend more time on them.

Carry out a review of your time regularly. Identify time stealers and make plans to remove them. Review your membership of professional organisations and other associations you belong to and check if they still meet your needs. Review your reading and your paperwork to identify what is helpful and what is just a burden.

Develop a simple system for organising your time and your key activities. Start from your goals and objectives and break them down into more manageable chunks. You may only need a diary, a to do list and a bring forward system, you may require something more sophisticated – but ensure that it requires relatively low maintenance.

Declutter your life and your work. William Spear in his book *Feng Shui Made Easy* states quite unequivocally: 'Get your desk or work station in order. Get rid of clutter and organise your files. Your desk will be a reflection of your brain'. Decluttering, however, is more than just your workspace – your bookshelves may be full of books that will never be read, your wardrobes full of clothes that will never be worn again (apart from at a 70s theme party!) and your garage full of tins and cans that you are very unlikely to use again. These may seem trivial but they take up time in finding the things that you really need and are always there as clutter – useless and chaotic, dissipating your energy and blurring your focus.

Build in time for personal recreation and exercise to ensure that you remain mentally and physically fresh to meet the challenge of working on your career goals. The great athletes and artists ensure that they are mentally and physically ready to follow their profession – this is an important principle for us all. Stephen Covey in *Seven Habits of Highly Effective People* reminds us that the more a saw is used the more it needs to be sharpened.

....

SUMMARY

The first two parts of *Plan Your Career* looked at where you are in your career and where you want to be. This part looked at how to get where you want to be.

As a first step, you looked at the path your career is taking and the path you would like it to take. A key element of career planning is to find a job that you love – a lot of time is spent at work, and as far as possible you want to enjoy it. This might mean taking advantage of the opportunities available to you within your current job; it might mean changing jobs; it might even mean changing career. For any of these options you will need to make the most of your opportunities, focus on your strengths, and get known by networking and 'selling' yourself.

It is important not to lose sight of the big picture – to take account of the wider implications of your job – and to simplify things so that you do not get bogged down with matters that take up time but lead you nowhere.

Plans will not, of course, necessarily go the way you want them to, since it is impossible to predict the future with accuracy. So you will need to prepare for uncertainties.

To get where you want to, and even to stay afloat where you are now, you will need to widen your set of skills. This is the subject of Part Four.

WHAT SKILLS WILL YOU NEED?

As the challenges in your industry or business grow, you may well need to widen your set of skills to ensure that you remain successful. Continuous development of your skills is a critical prerequisite of career success for the future. Once your skills become out-dated then you lose both your employability and your competitive edge. People aren't recruited because of their experience any more, they are recruited and promoted because of their skills and their ability to apply those skills flexibly.

There are three broad skill areas that most professionals and managers need to keep fully updated – professional/technical, business and personal competencies. All three skill clusters need to be kept up to date if you are going to achieve career success:

- professional/technical skills – because they form the basis of your expertise and your professional identity
- business skills – understanding the key elements of finance, marketing, IT, HR and the important ideas and concepts in business strategy
- personal competencies – the key personal skills that enable you to be effective at work:
  - analysis
  - creativity
  - decision making
  - personal impact
  - empathy
  - organisation
  - drive.

The three areas form a pyramid:

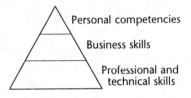

Personal competencies

Business skills

Professional and technical skills

....

PROFESSIONAL AND TECHNICAL SKILLS

Whatever your chosen career path, you have a set of professional or technical skills that have probably formed the basis of your success in your career. These skills will not be the only factor in your career growth but they will have formed an important part of it.

Your skills may be connected to a particular profession or industry, but they will need to be kept up to date and developed if they are to continue to support your career development. You have already identified your technical base, earlier in the book in Part One (page 20). An important task for the future is to make sure that this base is kept fresh and that you remain aware of the important trends in your chosen profession or business sector.

To a certain extent, when you move into more strategic levels in your organisation, you can leave the detail of your work to others, but you still need to ensure that you are in touch with the really important issues within your business or profession. You may not be required to act as a practitioner any more but you will need to have a good grasp of the key concepts and issues that are prevailing and are likely to shape the future ... your future. Your required knowledge and skill may move up to a higher level but it is still important to retain that connection with your profession.

How to keep up to date

- Read professional or business sector journals and papers.
- Attend meetings and conferences which involve leading edge ideas and concepts.
- Maintain a network of people who are in touch with new ideas – not only professional or business leaders but also new people coming through with new ideas and radical approaches to their work.
- Use commuting or waiting time to read books and journals on new concepts and new trends in your industry or profession.
- Talk to in-house specialists about their work.
- Use forums and Web sites to trawl the Internet for new ideas.

| GOLDEN RULE 19 |

To make progress, keep your skills up to date.

....

GENERIC BUSINESS SKILLS

The debate about generalists and specialists is becoming less of an issue. We are all becoming either generalist specialists or specialised generalists. The generalist needs to have a clear focus on where they can best apply their skills if they are not to become a jack of all trades. Equally the specialist needs to have a wider understanding about the business and its direction.

The two archetypes that are losing their currency are the 'super generalists' and the isolated specialist. The super generalist who can move from industry to industry and manage anything is becoming a rare phenomenon – although not totally extinct. Equally the specialist sitting in an office doing specialised things without any real reference to other people is a diminishing stereotype. Everyone needs to have areas of expertise in which they have really useful knowledge and the ability to understand their organisation well enough to know where that knowledge can usefully be put to work.

Everyone needs to have a set of business skills and wider business awareness in order to make a wider contribution to the business as a whole. These were touched on in Part One:

- customer service and marketing
- financial awareness
- IT literacy
- people management.

A checklist of skills was set out for each of these four categories on pages 23–4 and you should use these lists to ensure that you are aware of the key skills in each of these areas. These areas are important to your future development even if they are not part of the core of your work.

Customer service

Customer service is important for any member of an organisation. A real in-depth understanding of your organisation's customers and their needs is critical whether you are in a front-line role or in the furthest corner of the smallest backroom. Any business decisions that do not take the customer into account or support the customer proposition of the organisation will be counterproductive or irrelevant in the long term.

Financial awareness

Financial awareness is an important factor in any professional's role, even if they don't have direct financial accountability. An awareness of the costs and benefits of selecting different priorities is an important aspect of any commercial work. Professionals who cannot see the financial implications of their work will quickly be categorised as naive and uncommercial.

IT literacy

IT literacy is no longer a no-go area for anyone within the organisation – specialist or generalist. So many of our business processes are now on an IT system that it would be difficult to operate without good IT application skills and an awareness of the potential of IT to improve business processes. Increasingly information is passed across organisations through e-mail, the Internet and intranets, and they are so easy to use that even hardened technophobes can no longer claim exemption on grounds of complexity.

People management

People management is also important for ambitious people. Even without a large team of people it is important to know the key elements of people management and the organisation's human resource policy. This includes understanding the key principles of employment legislation and sensitivity to whatever industrial relations climate prevails in the organisation. It is also important to understand the main HR processes and to be aware of new developments in selection, assessment, management theory and development activities. This is important not only to be effective in your current role but also to be effective in the long-term management of your career.

Business understanding

Underpinning these four dimensions of business literacy is a wider understanding of the business world and the environment in which business is carried out. Business understanding involves the ability to scan widely across your industry, the market and the wider business environment in order to understand the key issues and trends that will have an impact in the future. This is important not only to enable you to make a greater contribution to your organisation in your present role but also to keep you aware of the key trends which may affect your future career growth. Business is a broad term in this context and is relevant even for people in organisations that are not primarily commercial – all organisations have customers, spend money, manage processes and develop people.

Business understanding involves the capability and motivation to think beyond the confines of your job and your own division or function to understand the organisation, the industry and the wider commercial environment and to take this wider knowledge into account when making decisions. People demonstrating high levels of this quality will be able to anticipate changes in their industry and will be able to predict the impact of trends on their future career development.

The overarching theme in developing business understanding is facing outward from your own department and looking across your organisation and your industry to spot new trends and ideas in order to ensure that your approach to work and business remains fresh and up to date.

Some useful tools and techniques for developing a wider perspective on business and organisations are outlined below.

Industry analysis

Michael Porter from Harvard Business School developed a process to help organisations analyse and understand their competitive environment. He believed that the state of competition in an industry depends on five basic competitive forces:

- the threat of new entrants into an industry
- the intensity of rivalry between existing competitors

- pressure from substitute products
- the bargaining power of buyers
- the bargaining power of suppliers.

This is a useful analysis for any competitive situation and can be used at a business unit or function level as well as for the organisation as a whole.

PEST analysis

PEST stands for Political, Economic, Social and Technological. It is a way of making sense of a complex world by identifying the key trends in the wider business environment. Scanning the environment regularly is a good way of keeping up to date with key trends and done systematically, linked with a more detailed industry analysis enables you to keep a handle on future developments and to build them in to your action plans.

The balanced scorecard

Robert Kaplan and David Norton recently developed a new approach to performance measurement – the balanced scorecard. Many performance measures highlight one area of a firm's activities (usually financial) at the expense of others; the balanced scorecard approach combines financial measures with operational, customer and capability measures. The process has the effect of breaking down strategic goals into a number of different areas and becomes the 'instrument panel' for the organisation. It is a useful tool to break down big strategic objectives into more detailed critical success factors supported by meaningful performance measures.

Developing business understanding

The tools and techniques outlined above can help to stimulate new thinking about the business and widen your horizon. In the long term, all managers and professionals need to develop a wider awareness about their own organisation and its environment. Even specialists need to have a more in-depth understanding of the context in which they carry out their profession and the management of business processes across organisational boundaries is becoming an important pre-condition of both organisational and individual success.

The following activities should help you to develop this approach:

- Find ways to introduce new ideas and discuss industry trends at your meetings. Many meetings are too closely focused on purely operational issues and need to have input on some broader and more strategic issues.

- Attend industry and professional conferences and then report back to your next team meetings about the key trends that you have discovered. Making a presentation to others will force you to think through some of the important issues rather than merely noting the key issues.

- Look for opportunities to work in other parts of the business, either on cross-functional project teams or for brief secondments; there is much evidence that these opportunities break down narrow functional mindsets and many organisations now insist that people work in at least two functions or sectors of the business before promotion to higher level roles.

- Check regularly on the progress of your business and your competitors, and be prepared to discuss business results in more detail with your colleagues in order to increase your understanding of the key business realities and the meaning underlying financial performance measures.

- Conduct an off-site strategic review with your team every year to identify key goals, critical success factors and priorities for the next year; ensure that this includes a review of industry and wider business trends.

- As well as your professional and organisational reading, read journals with a wider business and economic remit, such as the *Harvard Business Review*, *The Economist* and the *Financial Times*. Also read other political, economic or business journals occasionally such as *Fortune* and *Business Week*. American business journals are useful as they present a picture of how things happen in another business culture and often changes in US practice presage changes in the British experience.

- There are a range of books which highlight major social, economic, political and demographic trends and they can be particularly helpful in preparing businesses for the future – authors such as Faith Popcorn (*Clicking*), John Naisbitt (*Megatrends 2000*, *Asian Megatrends* and

Global Paradox), Francis Kinsman
(*Millennium*) and Hamish McRae (*The
World in 2020*) are all readable and
present a wider view of the future
although without any guarantee that they
will always be right! They look at the
world from new perspectives and identify
the implications of social and economic
trends.

✎ Use these questions as an indicator of the
   broader things you need to know in the
   future. If you can answer these, then you
   are demonstrating a good understanding
   of the wider business environment. If not,
   you may be working away in isolation
   from the important business trends. Be
   careful, the future may take you by
   surprise.

- What are your organisation's strengths and
  weaknesses?
- What are the key elements of its current
  strategy?
- What will your part of the business be like
  in five years' time? What are you doing to
  prepare for it?
- How do we know your part of the business
  is being successful? How will you measure
  its success?
- What are the key challenges facing your
  business in the next year?
- What are your competitors doing now in
  your area of expertise? Who are the new
  competitors and where will they come
  from?
- What is the 'future desired state' for
  your part of the business? How will

you get there? How will you know you
have been successful?

....

PERSONAL SKILLS

At the top of your pyramid are the personal
skills and qualities that enable you to be
successful. In Part One we clustered these into
thinking, relating and doing. Your own organisation may have a more sophisticated set of
qualities or 'competencies' that it believes are
necessary for future success, although my
guess is that they will reflect thinking, relating
and doing in some form or other. The qualities described here are the core skills that
underpin many competency frameworks.

Many people pay attention to professional
and business skills without looking to grow
and develop personally. Learning how to read
a balance sheet or to use PowerPoint for your
business presentations may be useful pieces of
additional knowledge, but the really important steps in our development are when we
learn to think more strategically or when we
develop a greater empathy and work more
productively with colleagues in other departments.

The following sections look at each of the
seven skill areas and identify ways to develop
them further. If one of these areas is already a
strength, then you will be able to sharpen
your performance even further and make it
into a real differentiator; if you feel that you
are weak in a particular area, then the evidence is that while you may not necessarily
turn it into a real strength, you may be able to
reduce its impact as a weakness.

Like sports or the arts, there are some people who possess natural skills and there are others who become effective through application and practice. The truly unbeatable are those who both have natural skills and work hard to develop them further. The most tragic are those who have natural skills but who waste them through lack of practice or application. The aim of this framework is to identify a balanced set of skills that are required for most organisational or professional tasks. They all need to be developed in some way for an individual to be truly effective in an organisational setting.

For example, effective problem solving at work is underpinned in some way by all the core qualities:

- good analytical skills to identify the cause of the problem
- creativity to generate some creative solutions
- decision making to select the option that fits the cause most closely under all the circumstances
- empathy to understand other people's perspectives on the problem and the likely solutions
- impact to persuade others of the importance of the issue
- drive to see the problem through to a solution
- organisation to develop processes and procedures to prevent the problem recurring.

The remainder of Part Four takes each skill in turn and shows how it can be developed and practised to enable you to be as effective as possible in the future.

ANALYSIS

The capacity to identify key issues and trends in complex problems.

The ability to appraise a situation, to break it down into its component parts and to draw conclusions from it is a critical skill as it enables all other activities to be based on a sound foundation of logic and reasoning.

At its foundation, analysis requires clarity of thought and the application of logic to routine problems. At its more strategic level, it involves analysing complex problems using data that may be incomplete or ambiguous.

Much of the development of analytical thinking comes from our education and upbringing. It has often been noted that thinking is not taught in British schools as a formal topic and tends to be approached as part of other subjects. Philosophers did the early work on analysis; in fact Descartes developed four rules for thinking in his book *Discourses on Method*:

- Never accept anything except clear and distinct ideas.
- Divide each problem into as many parts as are needed to solve it.
- Order your thoughts from the simple to the complex.
- Always check thoroughly for oversights.

These rules are still useful today and can form the basis of our approach to difficult problems or complex situations. It is important to emphasise that analysis should not be the only thinking approach used – it is always helpful to break issues down to solve them but we do sometimes require new insights to problems or opportunities which can only arise by reframing issues in an interesting and 'non-rational' way. There are a number of approaches to thinking which can help develop analytical ability and the following notes explain some of the situations that require analytical ability and briefly outline how they can be approached. They also include some questions to help stimulate your thinking.

Analytical ability can be developed by good questioning techniques. You should move into analytical thinking mode to ask yourself questions to stimulate your own thinking capability.

Situational appraisal

Understanding the key elements of a situation is an important first stage for good problem solving or decision making. This is also important for clear written communication – good writing is underpinned by clear thinking and the beginning of any report should state the situation and the key issues that the situation is intended to address. The key situational questions are:

- Define the situation – what are the key facts? What is happening? Who is involved?
- Identify complications – what issues need resolving? What is not happening as it should? What opportunities for action present themselves?

- Clarify the key questions – what are the real issues to be resolved? Are we problem solving, decision making or making a report or presentation?

Problem solving

Probably the most common application for analytical thinking is in the analysis and solution of problems – a process which involves asking a series of questions in a systematic way to come to a conclusion over the cause of a problem and find a solution which matches the cause. The key steps and the questions to ask for each are:

- **Step one: problem specification** – defining the true nature of the problem:
  - Where is the problem apparent? Where does it manifest itself? What adverse consequences are occurring that we want to remove?
  - How will you know when your problem is solved? What key question do you want your analysis to answer?

- **Step two: problem definition** – clarifying precisely the definition and location of the problem:
  - Where within the system/process/operation is the problem occurring? Where is it not occurring?
  - When does the problem occur and when doesn't it?
  - What happens when the problem occurs?

- **Step three: problem analysis –** understanding the likely causes of the problem and analysing these to find the most likely cause:
  - What is different about the location/timing/circumstances of the problem and the situation in areas where the problem does not exist?
  - What has changed recently which might make the problem arise?
  - What are the possible causes?
  - What is the most likely cause? Why do you believe that? Does it fit the information you have about the location of the problem? .

- **Step four: problem solution –** identifying a solution which most nearly resolves the problem by acting on its most likely cause rather than addressing the symptoms. At this stage the process turns into a decision-making process and the issues and questions set out above become particularly important:
  - What solution most closely fits our description of the problem?
  - What are the implications of choosing this solution above others?
  - What are the possible side-effects of selecting this solution?
  - Does the preferred solution fit with our analysis of the cause of the problem?

Analytical ability is an important skill as it forms the basis of others. Actions based on faulty logic are not likely to be successful. Although logic and reasoning alone are not enough to make a project successful, the lack of a firm logical basis can damage the project before it starts.

....

CREATIVITY

The capacity to look for alternative and unconventional ways to solve intellectual and practical problems.

Creativity is an important balance to analytical ability. It is now well recognised that while analytical thinking is a primarily left-brained activity, creativity is found in the right side of the brain – the side that recognises, among other things, music, art and emotions. The two need to be balanced in order to be fully effective but are rarely found as real strengths together in the same head. An important mix in team building is between analytical and creative thinkers – developing new ideas but on a base of sound logic. An unbalanced team can lead to either 'paralysis by analysis' or a mass of creative ideas that don't hang together in practice.

At its earlier stages, creativity involves identifying trends and recognising themes, making connections between different pieces of data; at more advanced levels, it involves reframing information and ideas to create new insights and encouraging people to look at things in new and unconventional ways in order to create completely new and original ways of working.

Creativity needs to be linked with business understanding in order to produce new business strategies. As the business world becomes more turbulent, the ability to understand and resolve complex problems becomes increasingly important and there are several ways to support the development of capability in this area – split into two categories:

- coaching tools and techniques to help you give some 'quick fix' help with a problem
- activities to support the individual in developing creative capability in the long term.

Tools and techniques to improve creativity

There are several approaches to creativity which have been developed to support individuals and organisations in their search to solve problems and develop new business opportunities; none of these techniques are completely comprehensive and none of them should be seen as a substitute for thinking. However, they are useful drills which if used in the right way can help you develop effective thinking habits which will enable you to deal more effectively with complex issues that require a more creative approach. Each technique is described in brief with references for further study, where available.

SWOT analysis

A SWOT analysis is simply a comparison of internal capability with external challenges. Strengths and weaknesses (SW) relate to internal capabilities and opportunities and threats (OT) relate to the challenges within the external environment. This technique is particularly useful when goals/objectives have been identified and priorities for action need to be agreed based on a succinct analysis of both internal and external factors. There are many descriptions of the technique but one particularly relevant description is in *Marketing Plans* by Malcolm McDonald and there is a brief Institute of Management checklist called 'Performing a SWOT Analysis', which describes how to carry out a SWOT analysis in a group setting. (To obtain a copy of the checklist, please write to the Institute of Management, Management House, Cottingham Road, Corby, Northants, NN17 1TT)

Force field analysis

Force field analysis is a simple technique to establish the forces which are likely to support a project or change initiative and those which are likely to oppose it; the approach involves clarifying the desired outcomes of an initiative and then identifying the factors which will move the initiative towards completion (these may be environmental, political, financial, social or relating to market trends) and which factors will cause the project to stall or fail. It can be used as the basis of a simple coaching session by asking an individual to identify supporting and opposing forces in any situation.

Scenario planning

A scenario is a description of what might happen in the future. Scenario planning is used to evaluate the outcomes of policies, plans and strategies in a range of different futures and is a way of testing the robustness of plans and strategies in the light of different possible futures. The technique was used extensively by Shell and has been described in a book by Arie De Geus (the former Shell strategic planning director) *The Living Company* and a further book by Peter Schwarz called *The Art of the Long View*. As we have seen earlier in the book, you can use basic scenario planning by asking for best/worst/most likely cases in potentially complex situations where the outcomes are not clearly known; this enables the individual to start building preventative and contingency plans for differing scenarios.

It also encourages greater creativity as it forces people to look at other ways of doing things and moves them away from the conventional way of thinking that is prevalent in most organisations – i.e. doing things the way we have always done them.

Stakeholder analysis

Stakeholders are people who have a 'stake' in a decision (i.e. the decision will have an impact on them) and who will probably influence both the nature of the decision and its implementation. Stakeholder analysis is a technique to help consider a problem from the various perspectives of its stakeholders and to identify how they might want the problem to be resolved. For example, a new product launch might be viewed from the perspective of the customer, the supplier, the distributor, the community as a whole, the end user and a range of other possible stakeholders.

You can use stakeholder analysis to encourage thinking about situations from different perspectives. Stakeholder analysis also has the effect of increasing empathy – another of our core qualities – by forcing yourself to examine an issue from someone else's viewpoint.

Reframing

The idea of reframing is to see things from a different perspective or within a different 'frame' or context. Different approaches to this can be to act as a 'devil's advocate' or to ask 'what if …?' questions. A simple example is to approach an issue from three perspectives: the first is to act as 'dreamer' to review the issues without constraints and visualise the full possibilities for an imaginative outcome; then act as a 'realist' to think about how the possibilities can be put into a practical action plan, and finally act as a 'critic' to criticise the plan in a constructive way. These approaches can be done with colleagues or alone. The three perspectives can be reiterated until an imaginative and practical plan has been developed.

Brainstorming

Brainstorming is a well-known technique aimed at idea generation rather than evaluation. It is more effective in a group setting and needs to be run carefully without early criticism or evaluation of people's contribution. Evaluation can be done later once a full range of interesting ideas have been established; if people evaluate too early, the less confident team members will hold back ideas that they perceive as having less value, thereby reducing the interesting options available to the team.

Edward de Bono's 'thinking hats'

Edward de Bono did much of the work to develop and popularise lateral thinking – that is, thinking that does not always follow the linear flow of 'vertical thinking'. A further development of his work has been his book *Six Thinking Hats*. It is a form of reframing – thinking about a topic in particular ways – and can be used to give a wider perspective on an issue. The six hats are:

- the **white** hat for neutral, objective and factual thinking ('Give me a summary of the facts'; 'Exactly what is happening here?')
- the **red** hat gives the more emotional view ('What is your gut feeling about the issue?')
- the **black** hat covers the negative aspects of why something can't be done ('What are the likely problems with doing it that way?')
- the **yellow** hat identifies possibilities and the positive reasons why something should be done (What new opportunities does this create for us?')
- the **green** hat indicates creativity and new ideas ('What is the most novel way to do this?')
- the **blue** hat is to do with control and organisation of the thinking process ('How should we be thinking about this?').

You can stimulate different types of thinking about an issue by asking yourself the questions set out in the brackets.

Mindmapping

Writing notes in a vertical, linear format can be very useful when we need to make a list in priority order, but can be unhelpful when we are trying to generate ideas in no particular order. Mindmapping – a technique developed by Tony Buzan – helps notetaking by using key words and images, set out radially rather than in vertical lines or columns. Issues are written down in a free flowing format without having to crystallise and organise information too quickly, and it is a great study technique.

Developing creativity

The tools and techniques set out above can help to generate new ideas and to look at things differently. In the long term, you need to develop your natural creative abilities so that you can think flexibly and strategically as a matter of course. The following activities should help to expand your creative thinking capability:

- Identify key figures, both inside and outside your business, whom you respect as creative and innovative thinkers. Examine their work and try to identify the techniques and approaches that they use to make radical changes in their function or industry.

- Don't limit yourself to reading business or technical journals. Read widely with a view to identifying important trends in the business world – what impact will they have on your industry and your career and what new ideas can be imported from outside into your own work. Try to read something that is unconventional and way outside your normal comfort zone – it may spark off some new ideas that you wouldn't see in your normal reading matter.

- Build in time in your own diary for

reflection and creative thinking – if you have a particular problem or issue, take time to consider the main components of the issue. Build time into meetings to review a major project and to look at how it could be managed differently.

- Stimulate yourself and your colleagues to think about the long term – what scenarios are possible within the business? How would you operate under each scenario?

- Avoid coming to conclusions too quickly during discussions about long-term strategy. Decisiveness is an important feature in operational matters but to be too quick to come to conclusions over important strategic issues can rob you of the opportunity to examine different alternatives or new scenarios and can prevent your team spending time identifying new approaches and learning how you make strategic decisions.

- Keep your own approach to business fresh – constantly look out for new ideas and learn new skills whenever possible; take opportunities to become involved and to involve your people in cross-functional project teams and training/development events – even those which do not have direct operational relevance to your own area of the business.

Questions to stimulate your creativity

When faced with an issue which requires more creative thinking, ask yourself:

- What possible ways are there of looking at this problem?
- How else might I/we approach it?
- What other opportunities are there in this project?
- What forces are working in my/our favour?
- What forces may work against me/us in this project?
- What are the best/worst/most likely scenarios – how would I/we approach this issue in each of these events?
- How am I/we thinking about this issue and how else can I/we think about it?
- Who are the key stakeholders and what is their perspective?
- What are the long-term consequences of doing it this way? What are the short-term implementation issues?

A mind that is stretched to a new idea, never returns to its original dimensions.

(Oliver Wendell Holmes)

DECISION MAKING

The ability to look at all the circumstances surrounding an issue and decide on a course of action.

Decision making is the third element of thinking that pulls together the other two skills and links them to relating and doing skills. It is moving away from 'pure' thought and looking to turn thoughts and ideas into action. Without decision making, analysis and creativity remain cerebral disciplines; with the ability to decide on a course of action they become the initial part of important projects and activities.

At foundation level, it involves identifying action plans for short-term activities and events; at more strategic levels it involves recognising and setting priorities for strategic opportunities or problems.

Activities for effective decision making

Improving decision making requires certain important activities:

- Make decisions between alternative courses of action to achieve a particular goal or objective.
- Identify the most critical priorities for action in a particular situation.
- Create an action plan with contingencies to ensure that decisions are put in place.
- Understand when to make decisions within a short time frame and when to make decisions based on the long-term needs of a situation.
- Act promptly and effectively in a crisis.

Who is good at making decisions?

The capacity and inclination to make effective decisions is often a factor of an individual's personality and conditioning. Some people are slow to make decisions, preferring to gather more information and weigh up the alternatives carefully. Others have a greater urgency and so tend to make their minds up quickly. Neither extreme is inherently good or bad. An important factor in decision making is knowing how urgent or important an issue is, and this leads to a decision on the priority of an issue based on both these factors.

The ability to make decisions is not purely a factor of high intelligence, although it is difficult to make effective judgements in a situation if you don't understand what is going on. People with high analytical or creative skills do not necessarily make good decisions and this is a bar to their personal effectiveness. It is not uncommon to meet someone with a powerful intellect but no real commercial sense – they are likely to remain specialists in a world that requires that good thinking is valuable only when it is converted into a coherent set of priorities and an implementation plan.

Developing the capability to make decisions

Learning to make decisions can be done as a matter of discipline. Learn to take decisions or set priorities in a systematic way until they become an automatic way of working. Some possible ways of developing this skill are:

• Ensure that any discussion ends with a clear agreement on the main actions that need to be taken. Often inaction is caused by not understanding what needs to be done from a mass of complex actions. If you can help to unpick this then you will have a clearer idea of the things that you need to do next.

- Create a sense of urgency about tasks with a clear deadline or target date for completion – any task without a deadline becomes a wish. Ensure that your deadline is sensible and achievable … with a stretch.

- Constantly review future trends and anticipate the future by developing action plans for likely future scenarios.

- Ensure that you and your team review experience on a regular basis, particularly in relation to crisis management. Whenever a crisis arises, identify the causes and re-run the event so that a more formal set of drills can be written and developed to ensure that future critical incidents are more effectively managed.

- Examine your daily activities list and separate the urgent priorities from the important. Good decision makers focus on the key issues in a situation and addressing those, not trying to deal with every element of a situation at once.

Decision making

Decisions are the critical points in your career. People forget your analytical ability and your creative skills but they will remember your decisions for a long time. Ben Heirs in his book *The Professional Decision Thinker* identified four steps for decision making. This is a good basis to think through your own approach to decision making.

Step one: the question

This step involves formulating or reformulating a question and gathering information relevant to answering that question. You need to ensure that the right question is being asked and that the right focus for the decision is being given. Ask:

- What are the key issues here?
- What factors need to be taken into account?
- What conditions need to be met?

Step two: the alternatives

This step involves creating the most effective range of alternative answers to the question posed in Step one. You must work to ensure that the most obvious option is not taken in haste for the sake of considering a range of alternatives that may generate a more productive decision. This depends on the importance and urgency of the decision – important issues need greater consideration and a wider range of options; urgent decisions require speed and the alternative that best fits the immediate requirements. Ask:

- What alternatives are there for this issue?
- How does each alternative meet the key issues – the things that the decision must resolve?
- What is the most useful alternative for action? Why are some alternatives discarded?
- How important is the issue? How urgent? How much time can be spent considering alternatives?

Step three: the consequences

For this step you must predict the future consequences of acting on each of the alternatives and creating the necessary plans to support each of them. Thinking through the alternatives, beyond their superficial attractions to their long-term consequences is critical for the long-term effectiveness of the decision. Ask:

- What would happen if we did ...? What would the consequences be? How attractive are these consequences?
- If we decide on a course of action, what contingency plans do we need to put in place to ensure a successful outcome?
- Do the consequences invalidate the decision? Are some of the consequences so dire that the benefits will not be achieved? What are the risks of certain actions – how critical are their consequences and how likely is the worst case scenario?

Step four: the decision

Use judgement to select the best alternative answer to the question posed with the best contingency plans to balance risk with reward. You must go through the decision systematically to ensure that the decision meets the original specification. Ask:

- What alternative most closely meets the requirements of the question?
- What alternative generates the most productive benefits?
- What alternative leads to the greatest risk?
- What are the possible consequences of action/inaction or delayed action?

Your current level of decision-making ability

✎ Ask yourself the following questions to check your current level of decision-making ability:

- What are the critical incidents that arise in your operation? How can you prevent them happening? How can you manage them more effectively when they arise?
- What are the key issues looming for the future? How will you resolve them?
- How quickly do you respond to emergencies and to the needs of your customers?
- How prepared are you to take risks? Do you wait until everything is perfectly planned before moving?
- Do your procedures encourage speedy action or do they hold things up by introducing unnecessary paperwork?
- Do you have a capacity to get things done? Do you respond quickly and with enthusiasm to new challenges?
- Do crises take you by surprise? Is there a set of procedures to go through to help anticipate them?

Life is not the way it is supposed to be. It's the way it is. The way you cope with it is what makes the difference.

(Virginia Satir, Psychologist)

PERSONAL IMPACT

The desire and ability to influence and motivate others to take action.

There are two key elements in the 'relating' cluster: impact – the capacity to influence and motivate others; and empathy – the ability to understand peoples' needs. Both elements are important in building effective working relationships. Impact without empathy is likely to result in one person dominating the relationship; empathy without impact is likely to lead to one person forsaking his or her own agenda at the expense of someone else's. Impact with empathy is a powerful combination and the basis for an adult-to-adult relationship with both parties able to state their own needs while retaining respect for the other's.

Impact is underpinned by a strong drive to achieve, as we shall explore in the 'Drive' section. People who want to make an impact need to have both the motivation and the influencing skills to enable them to state their own case powerfully while understanding and constantly checking the needs and perspectives of the other person.

This is particularly important in selling, and in your future career development you will always be selling something – your ideas, your career plans and the strategies of your business. Sales people need both empathy to help them understand the needs of their customers and impact to help them present their case in the most effective way. These two factors need to be supported by drive, which gives them the resilience to overcome barriers and continue to thrive in adversity.

Increase your impact

Impact is an important element of any influencing relationship. It is not as simple as 'charisma' because some very influential people are not charismatic; and some charismatic people are not as impactful as they might think they are! Developing impact is not easy, but there are activities that can help to increase your impact.

- Get feedback on your image, impact and style from your colleagues. You may wish to do this in a formal way by using a company 360° feedback process or you may prefer to do it informally. Be careful how you introduce this as many people don't like to be seen as giving negative feedback and may feel embarrassed about it.
- Identify opportunities to make presentations to others on your work – see yourself as 'on campaign' with a mission to raise awareness of your work and the key issues facing your team.
- Build up a good personal network and become a 'gatekeeper' to your colleagues, giving them access to your network.
- Spend time in thinking through an influencing strategy in your projects. Identify the key stakeholders and identify the right approach to gain their support.
- Look for interesting ways to present your work and learn to be an effective speaker. Presenting your work in an interesting and unconventional way is likely to increase your visibility and to add to your

level of impact. In a world full of 'suits' the person who stands out from the crowd will be remembered for much longer than the dull but worthy presenter, faithfully using the autocue to grind out one more speech on the organisation's strategy.

Each of us can work to change a small portion of events ... it is from numberless acts of courage and belief that history is shaped.

(Robert Kennedy, US Attorney General)

....

EMPATHY

The capacity to work effectively with other people by understanding their needs and motivation.

Empathy is not a soft quality; it involves reading people with sufficient insight to be able to motivate them, get things done and avoid potential problem areas. At its foundation level it involves active listening and appropriate responses; at higher levels it involves predicting potential responses and picking up very subtle signals.

✎ Empathy features in many corporate competency profiles. Some of its key features are described here. Measure yourself and your own people skills against them. The skills move from basic at the beginning to advanced towards the end of the list. Tick any description that you recognise about yourself; if your ticks are more concentrated at the beginning, then you need to work more on developing higher levels of empathy.

EMPATHY CHECKLIST

- ☐ Listens carefully and picks up the content and tone of voice of spoken communication

- ☐ Reflects back accurately comments from others to ensure understanding

- ☐ Listens openly and non-judgementally

- ☐ Makes time to pay attention and listen to others

- ☐ Is open to a range of viewpoints

- ☐ Understands unspoken or poorly expressed meanings as well as what is actually said

- ☐ Recognises obvious body language signals

- ☐ Strives to understand the reasons behind people's actions

- ☐ Picks up non-verbal signals and changes style or approach accordingly

- ☐ Asks open questions to try to understand situations better

- ☐ Predicts and prepares for other people's reactions to events

- ☐ Anticipates responses to communications by interpreting present and past behaviour

- ☐ Responds to people's concerns by adjusting

their own behaviour in a helpfully
responsive manner

☐ Picks up on subtle signals in group
meetings or one-to-one to predict likely
outcome of discussions

☐ Is easy to approach with difficult or
sensitive issues

☐ Shows ability to put themselves in the
other person's position and anticipate their
likely approach to a topic

☐ Able to take a balanced view of individual
strengths and weaknesses and use that to
frame an effective approach

☐ Understands other people's underlying
problems and the reasons for current or
habitual behaviour

☐ Demonstrates a maturity of judgement in
dealing with difficult or sensitive issues

☐ Is able to provide support without taking
over the individual's problem or backing a
particular solution

☐ Thinks and acts from the other person's
values and beliefs

☐ Develops a strong awareness of the other
person's interests and motives

☐ Is prepared to bring sensitive issues into the
open and to deal with them objectively
and without bias or prejudice

☐ Deals effectively with several people's
differing motives, interests and values
during one event

Developing empathy

It was once flippantly said about sincerity that 'once you could fake that, you could fake anything'. Many people assume the same about empathy, believing that it is a set of techniques that help you manipulate people and bring them round to your way of thinking. The least empathetic person I have ever worked with, regularly asked people how they felt, and thought that this was empathy in action.

Empathy is rooted in a strong desire to see things from the other person's perspective. It is the basis of good working relationships based on mutual trust and understanding and is not a superficial technique for persuading or manipulating others. Some of the following points should help to develop a greater understanding of yourself and your approach to people as well as developing your own capacity for understanding and valuing the needs and values of others.

Do the following to help you develop empathy:

- Make a list of your major prejudices – personality types, behaviours, topics on which you have strong opinions – these will be the barriers to your thinking. Make a conscious effort to control these prejudices when you meet them at work.

- Get feedback from colleagues when you have had a discussion with them – ask if you gave them enough airspace.

- Practise reflecting back feelings to people.

- Become a people watcher – enjoy interpreting their body language and their tone of voice. In meetings, watch people carefully and try to identify what they are feeling and anticipate their approach during the next discussion.

- Develop a good working relationship with someone you don't like or someone who has a different approach to life and work.

- Learn to take your own emotional temperature – monitor your own responses and feelings regularly, particularly on contentious issues.

✎ Take a complex issue you are dealing with now – one that involves some complex 'political' issues. Write down a list of the parties involved and describe their issues and motives. Plan how you will address the issue while still respecting their values.

✎ Reflect on an issue where you failed to gain commitment. What were the key interpersonal issues? How did you tackle them? How could that have been improved?

✎ Ask yourself the following questions to help you to focus on the development of empathy from your perspective:

- Where do you 'lose the plot'? Where do your prejudices stop you listening effectively to others?
- How does your personal style impact on other people – do you dominate or hold back?
- How comfortable are you in discussions about people's feelings?
- How well do you know how people feel

about particular issues? How much is hidden and how much is visible with careful observation?

- What type of people do you relate well to? What types do you find more difficult? Why?
- What are the key issues that you are facing? What are your beliefs and values in relation to this issue? What are the beliefs, values and motives of others?
- How well do you think through other people's responses to issues? What method do you have for ensuring that you do this?
- Where do you face the most opposition? How well do you understand why?
- How do you get feedback about your style and approach?

....

ORGANISATION

The ability to get things done by effective planning and organising.

Organisation is a critical competency for people at work today. It is no longer a 'nice to have' in a complex world where every project requires the coordination of increasing numbers of people and processes. People start by planning and organising their own work effectively; at higher levels, it involves developing an infrastructure for the delivery and monitoring of high quality work and the provision of good information systems.

There are two key issues with organisation – one is the need to manage individual projects and activities effectively; the other is to manage a portfolio of activities by setting priorities and allocating time on the basis of importance and adding value.

Managing a project or task

Before working on a project or task, ask yourself:

- Why is this piece of work being done?
- How will its success be measured?
- Who is the end user? What are their needs?
- What vision of the finished product do I have?
- What issues/problems will this work resolve?
- Who needs to be involved in the decision making?
- Who needs to know the plans?
- What is the deadline? When does it need to be completed?
- What are the critical dependencies? What other activities does it/can it link with?
- What priority does this work have? Is it important or urgent?
- What are the key milestones for the work?
- How will the work be monitored?
- What information is required? Where will it come from?
- How clear are people's objectives? Are they specific and measurable?
- What review mechanisms are in place? How will good practice be spread?
- How will people learn effectively from the work?
- How will we ensure that we have the

capability to carry out the work?
• How will the activity be linked into other pieces of work?

Managing time

Another key issue is the management of time – setting priorities and identifying the important and the urgent issues. Urgent issues are normally responding to external stimuli that need to be dealt with quickly; important issues are often self-initiated tasks that need to be dealt with effectively. The following matrix taken from Stephen Covey's *First Things First* identifies how time is spent.

Check your use of time

✎ Ask yourself the following questions to identify your use of time.

• In which quadrant do you spend most of your time? Complete a simple time log for a week and identify the location of your work on the matrix?
• **For the urgent work** – what crises could be prevented? Would some 'important time' help to prevent them?
• What work can be delegated – mainly the urgent/not important quadrant?
• **For the important work** – how much time is spent in the important/not urgent quadrant where the high quality work for the future is done?
• How can you find time for more important work?
• When is the best time to do this work?

- **For the non-important and non-urgent work** – which parts of this work can you delegate or drop altogether?

	Urgent	Not urgent
Important	**Fixing the present** • Crises • Pressing problems • Deadline driven meetings, projects and preparations	**Shaping the future** • Preparation and planning • Personal development • Relationship building • Scanning the business environment • Thinking time • Recreation
Not important	**Maintainence** • Interruptions • Some phone calls, some mail, some reading • Routine operations	**Trivia** • Trivia • Junk mail • Casual socialising – as opposed to relationship building • Time wasters • Displacement activity

Source: *First Things First*, S. Covey, 1994

How time is spent

Remember that work can be handled in five ways:

Done – focus on the most important things and make sure you do them yourself.

Delegated – delegate things that others can do more effectively than you can.

Diverted – find other ways to do some of your less important tasks: outsourcing, subcontracting etc., particularly for the urgent/not important quadrant tasks.

Dumped – stop doing the 'neither urgent nor important' work. Challenge the relevance and viability of work of this nature. It is probably stopping you doing something really important.

Drills – introduce some brief routines which enable less important work to be despatched quickly and effectively.

Identify which parts of your work can be placed in each category.

....

DRIVE

Persistence in pursuit of stretching objectives, overcoming difficulties and barriers.

The concept of drive is an important factor in getting things done in a complex organisation and in a competitive world. It has three important components – courage, achievement orientation and tenacity – which are personal qualities that underpin some of the other competencies. In the 'iceberg' of successful people, they are hidden well below the surface, forming the basis of success in other competency areas. This means that they are closely tied up with some of the more complex elements of individual personality and character and so may be more difficult to develop if you feel that they are not an integral part of your set of qualities.

The key to developing drive is not necessarily through formal development processes but through the slow but steady building of character and initiative within the individual. This can be done by exposing yourself to different business experiences not only to learn new skills but also to develop the courage and confidence to tackle increasingly difficult organisational issues.

There is a view that some of these qualities are born and not made. It is true that some people are naturally predisposed to have courage and personal drive, due often either to their genetic inheritance or to their early life experience. However, these qualities can be developed and with care and the right approach can be brought out in each individual to varying degrees. As the business world becomes more turbulent, it becomes more critical to develop them in order to enable the business and the people within it to survive and thrive.

Courage

Courage is the quality that enables you to take personal risks to accomplish tasks or to challenge more senior managers and to look to change organisational norms and identify new ways of working.

• Identify ways to challenge business activities that you feel are unhelpful or unproductive. Don't feel constrained by organisational conventions and strictures about the right way to do things. Equally, be aware that there may be some of your colleagues who are closely aligned to the status quo; be careful how you tackle them and work hard to win them over to your view. Temper your courage with empathy.

• Set yourself stretching objectives and work hard to achieve them. Don't fall back on making small improvements, but focus on making really significant changes to your performance and contribution to the organisation.

• Practise speaking out on issues on which you feel strongly. Once you get used to it, you will find it easy to speak out assertively but without aggression on topics which are important to you.

Avoiding danger is no safer in the long run than outright exposure. The fearful are caught as often as the bold.

(Helen Keller)

Achievement orientation

Achievement orientation is based in a pride in setting and exceeding your own standards.

• Spend time in setting goals and keep setting yourself more ambitious goals and targets; aim for things that are attainable but at a real stretch.

- Review performance regularly. Where targets are achieved with ease, identify new targets so that you are always aiming higher.

- Celebrate success and make it a matter of pride to achieve stretching personal goals; don't punish yourself or your team for failure in pursuit of a challenging goal, it will act as a disincentive to go for more stretching goals in the future. Reserve your criticism for those people who don't strive for ambitious targets and who are prepared to do the minimum required.

Tenacity

Tenacity is the determination to overcome obstacles in pursuit of stretching goals. In the management of your career it will be one of your most important qualities. However, it is important to clarify that tenacity is not the mindless repetition of an unsuccessful strategy. If something isn't working, try something else. Tenacity without, for example, good thinking skills or empathy is a poor strategy, likely to end in failure.

- Before each project do a force field analysis (see page 148) to identify the forces which may work against the project and work to prevent the problems arising.

- Break down major goals into do-able increments, review progress regularly and allow your projects to develop a momentum for success. The achievement of several smaller steps leads to increased confidence and morale, so that you can tackle the more difficult tasks with greater self-assurance.

- Keep yourself fit and maintain a balanced life outside work. Tenacity is not the dogged pursuit of almost unachievable objectives; it involves maintaining the energy and enthusiasm to meet and overcome obstacles in the pursuit of stretching business and personal goals. Keep your energy levels high by good diet and regular exercise.

- Learn to relax more so that when a real crisis arises you are able to sustain long working hours and still keep a clear head. Most business issues are fundamentally unimportant when compared to the really critical issues in life – your health, your family and your friendships. Maintain a detached perspective about what you do at work – learn to stand back from it occasionally and review it as if you were an external consultant.

Far better is it to dare mighty things, to win glorious triumphs, even though chequered by failure, than to take the ranks of those poor miserable spirits who neither enjoy much nor suffer much because they live in the grey twilight that knows neither victory nor defeat.

(Theodore Roosevelt, American President)

PERSONAL DEVELOPMENT PLANNING

The way to develop effectively in a busy world with competing priorities is to put together a plan to develop the skills and knowledge you need. Everyone at work needs to have a clear plan to refresh their reservoir of skills and knowledge. Every business needs to pay equal attention to strategy and capability – likewise, a key part of your career strategy must be aimed at developing your capability to operate effectively in the future.

Much of the data for your development plan has already been gathered and in this section we will be pulling this together to help you develop a clear action plan.

Your development plan will be made up of the following elements:

- actions to enhance the strengths which you identified earlier in the process
- actions to resolve the weaknesses identified during the process
- a plan to develop the new skills required to help you in future roles
- a plan to help you anticipate the skills that your business will require for the future.

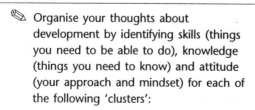 Organise your thoughts about development by identifying skills (things you need to be able to do), knowledge (things you need to know) and attitude (your approach and mindset) for each of the following 'clusters':

- technical and professional – the specialist skills you need to have to be more effective within your own profession
- business – the skills of management that all professionals require: marketing, customer service, financial awareness and IT
- personal – the 'enabling' competencies that differentiate truly effective performers.

✎ Now take each of these clusters and identify your core needs for additional skill, knowledge and approach for each of them.

✎ Think how you might resolve some of these development needs. There are a range of training and development options available – not necessarily course based – and you may wish to discuss these in more depth with your human resources or training manager. Some of the options are listed below. Tick those you think might be right for you.

☐ Training courses – in-house or external. External programmes give an added perspective to your work by meeting other professionals from different organisations or business sectors

☐ Personal coaching from your line manager

☐ Personal coaching from an in-house functional specialist, or an external coach or mentor

☐ Distance learning, via workbooks, CD-ROM, interactive video, audiotapes and books

☐ Education programmes, such as MBA, DMS or a professional development activity

- ☐ Benchmarking visits overseas or to customers/suppliers

- ☐ Networking with external specialists and internal colleagues from other departments

- ☐ Joining a professional institute and attending their meetings

- ☐ Undertaking a 360° feedback programme

The important issue with development planning is to have a clear objective of what you want to achieve from the activity – set yourself some clear development objectives to focus your attention on the key learning points. You only have so much time and energy to spend on your personal development, so spend your time on the things that will bring you closer to your personal goals.

SUMMARY

You need never stop learning or developing. You will need to keep your skills updated as you progress in your career, so that you can move forward but also so that you do not fall behind.

The areas you will particularly want to keep updated are your professional and technical skills, your business skills, and your personal competencies. In this section we have talked about how you may keep your skills up to date and looked in some depth at the seven core personal skills: analysis, creativity, decision making, empathy, personal impact, drive and organisation.

You should now be in a good position to know what skills you need to update and how to go about it. Your personal development plan is a working document that you should bear in mind when you are doing your yearly, quarterly, monthly and daily plans we looked at in Part Two.

The final part of *Plan Your Career* brings together all the rules this book has introduced and suggests actions you can take to follow them.

Part five

ACTION PLANNING

Make career management a life-long habit for life-long success.

Many people regard career management as a one-off hit. The most common form of career review is the outplacement programme which people undergo when they have been made redundant. This may not be the best time for a full-scale review because the important driver at this time is to get quickly back to work and so there is less time to consider a wide range of career options. Once outplacement participants have found a new job, they are so relieved that they want to forget anything to do with their period of redundancy and just get on with their lives again.

Career management is still not a regular feature of organisational life, since many businesses want to avoid creating an opportunity for their key professionals to think through their career options. Their fear is that their high potential people will find a more attractive alternative elsewhere and so they prefer to keep any career discontent suppressed.

However, career management is an important feature of working life for both the individual and the organisation. For the individual it is important to monitor your career success and keep a careful eye both on opportunities to grow and some of the important trends in your organisation or profession. For the organisation it is a good opportunity to review individual contributions, capability and career development to make sure that your key people are performing to their full potential. It also helps to uncover any dissatisfactions or frustrations at an early stage rather than let them grow to a size that makes them more difficult to manage.

Career management therefore must be for life and, to paraphrase the RSPCA advert, 'not just for Christmas'. It is not a one-off hit but a key process which enables you to keep track of your development in relation to the changing economic and social environment. The world is changing so much now that you have to remain alert for new opportunities (and new threats) all the time. Career management is the personal development equivalent of preventative medicine – like the Chinese medical tradition, the aim of good career management is to keep you well, not to heal you when you are sick. You should be keeping ahead of the game, not be playing 'catch up'.

THE GOLDEN RULES

Throughout *Plan Your Career* there are twenty golden rules for career management. They are all things that need to be done for career survival in the new millennium. The following notes suggest some key actions for you to take now and in the future to enable you to meet your career goals.

Rule 1.
Successful career planning begins with understanding your skills and motivations

The most important piece of knowledge we ever acquire is knowledge about ourselves and what makes us effective and successful. Too often we are too busy working and living to stand back and understand what makes us tick – why are we successful at some things or in some circumstances and not others? There are some important things you need to know about yourself at work:

- What are you really good at? What are your main strengths?
- What are you really bad at? What are your limitations?
- What motivates you? What are the drives and values that make you seek out certain types of work?
- Under what circumstances do you deliver your best work? When have you felt particularly 'in flow'?

Actions

- Carry out a regular review of your skills and values against whatever competency profile is in place within your business.
- Use any formal or informal mechanisms you can to gain feedback on your performance or capabilities – ask for detailed feedback at your appraisal, go through a programme of 360° feedback if one is available (ask your HR manager if none is available), and ensure that you have clear measures of performance in place.
- Benchmark yourself against others within your own organisation or your own profession. Set your benchmarks high and don't limit yourself to the most obvious comparators – measure yourself against the best in your class.

Rule 2.
Look back and learn from your successes and failures

Before looking for more sophisticated forms of feedback, you should normally reflect back on your career for information about your skills and abilities. You have come to this book with a track record of achievement in a range of different commercial situations; you also have a wealth of experience in activities which while not work-related are relevant to your working life.

This is all important information for your future career development. You are likely to be more successful if you are doing things that you enjoy. The process of self-appraisal involves examining your background and experience to identify where you have a sense of genuine achievement and where you have genuinely felt 'in flow', completely absorbed by the task in hand.

It involves answering the following questions:

- What key abilities or personal qualities have enabled you to reach your current position?
- What are your main achievements at work or elsewhere?
- What do you most enjoy doing?
- Under what circumstances have you been most successful?

Actions

- Carry out regular reviews of your successes and failures. When something goes well, identify the reasons for your success, and try to build those elements into future projects; when something goes wrong, try to identify the reasons and build those conclusions into your future plans.
- Find someone you know well and develop a 'peer coaching' relationship with them so that you can learn together with someone who is more detached and can ask you the difficult questions that you might avoid yourself. Find someone who is not in your own business or profession, who is not competing with you and is able to provide non-directive support.

Rule 3.

Look ahead and think clearly about where you want to be

The world of work has become much more complex in the last few years – every sector of the economy, both public and private, has undergone massive change. This is not a passing phase, so those people who are just waiting for things to get back to normal are going to be disappointed. In a time of radical change, many people give up on their goals and become fatalistic about the future, allowing themselves to float like a cork on the surface of the sea, keeping afloat but drifting with the tide.

In fact, during times of change and complexity, a clear goal for your career becomes much more important if you are to be successful. Instead of being the victim of difficult circumstances, the person with clear goals uses them as a compass and maintains their sense of direction and purpose, moving towards a well-defined future. Sometimes, these goals need to be followed with some flexibility as the strategy for achieving them will need to be adjusted with changing circumstances. However, a clear set of goals is an important outcome for any career review or career plan. Important questions about goals will be:

- Do you have a clear set of things that you want to achieve at work?
- How far have you progressed in achieving these?
- What are the next key steps for moving towards these goals?
- How will you measure your progress?
- Where do you want to be in five years, ten years, twenty years ...?

Actions

- Review your progress towards your goals on a regular basis (at least every ninety days) and spend some time each week identifying things that you need to do to move more quickly towards them.
- Carry out a full review of your goals annually to ensure that they still remain relevant. Write them down and keep them in a safe place and in a form that you can review them easily and regularly. They are an important part of your future success and should be the template for your activities.

Rule 4.

Balance your work with the rest of your life

The prime purpose of work is to enrich your life and not to dominate it. Work should enable you to improve the quality of your life and not leave you frustrated and unfulfilled. There are many strategies which are being adopted to improve this balance – the current increase in books about 'downshifting' is an indication that fewer people are finding their fulfilment in the remorseless grind of work.

The answer to finding the balance is to see your work as one part, albeit a particularly important one, of your life. Whole life consists of family, recreation, friends, health and community as well as work. If work is all we have, life loses much of its meaning and, in the long term, our work suffers too as we don't do the things that 're-create' ourselves, and like a machine that is not properly serviced, we break down and lose our edge.

Actions

- Carry out the Life Balance exercise regularly to check that you are keeping the important elements of your life in balance.
- Learn to read the signs of stress more closely. Stress may be a sign that you are spending so much time in one part of your life that you are neglecting some of the other elements.
- See diet, exercise and relaxation as an important part of your career management regime. See yourself as a corporate athlete and aim to keep yourself in good condition for the challenges ahead.

Rule 5.
Focus on a career path, not just a job

The job is of less importance in today's market than the career path. As the world of work changes, the job is becoming an increasingly transient phenomenon; every restructuring leads to a change in job definitions. I recommend that you don't hold too tightly on to your job but that you do take your choice of career path very seriously and keep your path in mind when you make career decisions.

Actions

- Identify the key things that you need to do to achieve your career goals – the skills, experience and activities. Work out a plan to ensure you achieve them.
- Work on the plan and define it before discussing it with your line manager or

your HR manager. It is important to gain other people's support for your career plans, particularly people who can help you make them happen. If your current manager is unable to support your plans, you must try to identify their concerns, but you shouldn't use this as an excuse to shelve your plans. Your manager may not wish to lose you and your HR department may have plans for you that don't fit your own career goals. Be assertive in these situations and ensure that your own agenda, not theirs, is discussed.

Rule 6.

For career success, find a job that you love

One of the enduring Greek myths that has such relevance today is the myth of Sisyphus, condemned in Hades to push a large stone uphill, only to see it constantly roll back down again. In *The Myth of Sisyphus* Albert Camus (1942) described his fate thus:

> *The gods had condemned Sisyphus to ceaselessly rolling a stone to the top of a mountain, whence the stone would fall back of its own weight. They had thought with some reason that there is no greater punishment than futile and hopeless labour.*

Many people today are working ceaselessly at a job that they see as 'futile and hopeless'. Organisations have a responsibility to create meaning in the work people do so that it becomes useful and fulfilling; equally, employees have a responsibility of their own – to vote with their feet! If your job is boring and

unfulfilling, then change it or leave it. You
will never be successful in a job that is dull and
meaningless.

Actions

- Do the 'Sunday evening test': does the
  prospect of the next week fill you with
  horror, or enthusiasm? If it fills you with
  horror, identify changes to your job
  which will make it more attractive and
  will enable you to learn new things; even
  if your job fills you with enthusiasm, you
  can still find ways to make it even more
  enjoyable and keep looking for new ideas
  to do it even better.
- If it still fills you with horror or it looks
  like a career cul-de-sac, make plans to
  leave. Think very carefully about what
  you really want to do, then write your
  CV, contact your network, ring
  headhunters and start looking closely at
  the newspapers. Whatever happens, don't
  stay in a job that you hate. Read *Job
  Seeking* by Karen Holmes, also in the
  Career PowerTools series.

Rule 7.

Look for organisations where your skills can be developed

Only look for situations where you will grow
and develop. Every move has to be analysed in
terms of the enhancement of your CV –
interesting projects, the opportunity to
develop new skills, your organisation is seen as
a market leader or a sector leader within your
specialism. The key question for each career

move, internally or externally, must be 'What value does this add to my employability?'

Actions

- Make sure that you work for an organisation that helps you learn new things and gives you new challenges. Check this out at the interview – your development is more important in the long term than your remuneration package and yet receives far less attention.
- Focus on your CV. Ask yourself if your current job is enhancing your CV, not in the cosmetic sense, but is it adding to your stock of interesting and challenging experiences. Are you growing and contributing, or are you marking time? If you are marking time, then you are going backwards in real terms.

Rule 8.

To be successful you must focus on your strengths and manage your weaknesses

An important rule is to focus on your strengths, they will always be the source of your success. If you can do more of what you are good at then you will always increase your productivity and become more successful.

Observe really successful people in professions such as sport or the arts – they take their skills and hone them to world-class performance, rather than trying to be all-rounders. No one expects the world-class violinist to be able to play the bassoon, just in case the bassoonist doesn't turn up. The great instrumentalists choose their instrument with care and then devote their career to becoming the best in their class.

You must, however, develop strategies to minimise your weaknesses, particularly those weaknesses which reduce your ability to make your strengths productive. Your strategy may be to find someone with complementary skills or to develop new skills yourself, but if you know that a particular weakness is holding you back, then work hard to find a way to minimise it.

Actions

- Identify your five core strengths and brainstorm ways to make them more productive for you. Identify ways in which you can make them work harder for you.
- Identify your five main weaknesses and identify ways to manage them more effectively in order to reduce their negative impact.

Rule 9.

Get out more and expand your network

One of the key skills for career management is the ability to form and maintain a network of people who we can work with and learn from. The business world is diverse and unpredictable; managers and professionals are being told that they are now responsible for their own career. Networking, forming effective working relationships with others, is one way for the individual to mitigate the effects of this more complex world – not just to find people who can help them 'get on', but also to find people who can introduce them to different ways of working or can help them make the most of their strengths by providing complementary skills.

Networking is much more than the ritual exchange of business cards at a conference and an occasional telephone call; it requires the ability to form productive and reciprocal working relationships with people who can provide support, new ideas or a different perspective. It takes away the feeling of 'mission impossible' that so many people at work seem to have, when they feel that they are working on a solo mission in hostile territory, without support or guidance.

It also requires a high degree of skill and an investment of time but with excellent returns. It is a skill which is helpful not only in career terms but also in your personal and community life. We are still social animals and people who can develop good, proactive networking skills will find life and work not only easier but also more enjoyable.

Actions

- Make a list of your key contacts and identify which of your networks they belong to. Make sure you know where they are now and ensure you have contact numbers.
- Draft a plan to keep yourself up to date with your existing network. Make four or five calls a week to keep in touch, and try to meet up with those you really want to keep in close contact with. Aim for one networking meeting a week. It is an important investment in your career development.
- Identify people who you would like to

contact or feel would be a positive addition to your network. Attend conferences or professional meetings and identify people who you would like to meet. Then introduce yourself to them.

Rule 10.

Know when to make a career change

The S-curve theory of change describes all change as starting slowly, growing and developing until reaching a peak and declining – this is possibly the story of most institutions, trends, products and relationships. It is also the story of most careers – you move into a job, develop slowly … then a little faster before becoming fully proficient and then falling victim to the 'law of diminishing returns', before a final decline.

Usually something happens to start a new curve; a new challenge, a change of ownership in your business or a sudden increase of responsibility gives fresh impetus and you start developing new skills to meet the challenge. However, if no new challenge appears, it is essential that you actively seek one either inside or outside your business. Staying on a downward curve for too long is immensely damaging for your career, your motivation and self-esteem; you forget how to meet a challenge and you become stale and unproductive.

Maintaining the momentum of growth and development is a critical career strategy – changes on the S-curve are easier to make on the way up than they are on the downward slide; recovering from a point of stagnation is the worst of all worlds and takes a super-human effort of will.

Actions

- Stand back and review your career to date. When have you recognised the signs telling you that you are ready for a move? How are you feeling about these now?
- Draw up your personal S-curve. What is your current curve like and where are you on it? What is the future curve like? How near are you to wanting to make a move from one to the other?

Rule 11.

To make progress break out of your comfort zones

Related to the S-curve rule, is a rule about comfort zones. As soon as you are relaxed and comfortable in a job, change it! You need to be feeling slightly uncomfortable if you are to succeed and grow in the modern business world. You can make yourself uncomfortable by changing jobs, setting yourself more stretching goals or objectives, working in a different area of the business where you need to develop a new set of skills.

Actions

- Examine your current career goals. Are they truly stretching or just more of the same?
- How are you feeling about your work? If you feel comfortable, then you are not

stretching yourself enough! Try to identify some activities at work that will make you uncomfortable and learn to manage that discomfort. Learn some new things outside work to keep yourself fresh and maintain your creative edge.

Rule 12.

Be alert for opportunities within your current role

Building a track record of success in your current role is an important career strategy. Excellent performance in your current role enables you to become more visible without unnecessary self-promotion and provides you with a track record which can form the basis of your career growth.

Many organisations have conducted extensive delayering exercises and this has increased the size of jobs and the space between one job and the next higher level. This has increased the scope for expansion within the job rather than growing through moving between jobs. The delayered organisation requires people who, using their own initiative, see the job description as the core of the job, a base for further exploration rather than the job itself.

Actions

- Stand back and identify five opportunities in your current role where you can make significant improvements in contribution.
- Identify five places in your current job where you can learn new skills or gain fresh experience.

Rule 13.

Seek more influence on critical decisions

Edgar Schein, a notable academic writer on career growth, identified three directions for career dynamics: upwards (promotion), sideways (broadening/development) and inclusion – moving from the periphery to the centre. It is this third option that is least acknowledged: moving towards a position of greater influence and greater centrality within the organisation or the profession.

Seeking a greater involvement in the key decisions within the business is an important career management strategy. It increases not only your level of influence within the organisation but it increases your awareness of what is going on within the business and enables you to do more effective scenario planning, based on more useful data about the future and your organisation's intentions.

Actions

- Identify five important issues in your current role where you would like to have more influence. Draft a plan to make sure you get that influence.
- Who are the people who have real influence on the way things are done in your part of the organisation? Make sure they are on your contact list very soon.

Rule 14.

Plan ahead – prepare for an uncertain future

The world we are working and living in now is complex and unpredictable and we all need to come to terms with that uncertainty if we are to survive and flourish in the future. One way that large organisations prepare for uncertainty is by scenario planning – a technique which identifies a range of possible futures and creates plans and policies to cope with each eventuality. Of necessity, some of these outcomes will not arise, but the organisation will be ready for them if they do and, in any case, will have raised their level of adaptability to changing circumstances and thereby increased their confidence about meeting future challenges.

The technique of scenario planning is also appropriate for the individual in preparing for an uncertain future. Many employees have been taken by surprise by a sudden change in company strategy and have found their career aspirations in tatters because they had no alternative career plan.

Actions

- Identify three career scenarios – growth, retrenchment and business as usual. What opportunities or threats do these scenarios present to you?
- After reviewing the scenarios, identify new ways of working to take into account the things you have learned from them. How can you maximise the opportunities from the growth scenario and minimise the threats from the retrenchment scenario?

- Identify four ways to keep in closer touch with the external business environment.

Rule 15.
Ride trends, not fads

The future is in the hands of those who can predict and anticipate it. Given a choice between making it happen, watching it happen and wondering what happened, you must be in the 'making it happen' role. Those people who make it happen may not necessarily be the visionaries but are those who see things occurring and are able to understand how best to turn them to their own advantage.

It is important to recognise the difference between a trend and a fad. A trend is a significant change in either social, economic or technological realities (e.g. the ageing population), whereas a fad is a transient fashion which waxes and wanes quickly (e.g. total quality management, flares, empowerment). Observe trends carefully and work out what they mean for your own business or profession, then do something with the information.

Actions

- Identify five important trends within your profession or industry that could have an impact on the way you work in the future. Note down how they will effect you and develop an action plan to enable you to prepare effectively for them.
- Read a business journal and identify some likely wider business or social trends that

will have an impact on you and your work. Ask yourself what you are doing to prepare for them.

Rule 16.

To be successful you must be your own marketing consultant

Psychologists claim that perception is reality – that how people perceive things is as important as the reality. Managing your career involves taking care of both the reality and the perception. You have to have both the sausage and the sizzle if you are to make your mark in today's workplace! Pay attention to your image, how people see you and how they describe your brand identity. No amount of image management can rescue a poor track record, but poor perception can undo years of hard and productive work.

Actions

- Ask a supportive friend or colleague how you are perceived – what is your 'brand identity'?
- Take the opportunity to undergo some psychometric tests and get feedback from the assessor (the Myers Briggs Type Inventory is very useful for this). Note down the main messages and outcomes and check these out with a friend or member of your family.
- Identify three opportunities to make pesentations about your work to others within your organisation. Make sure

the presentations are professional and well prepared.

Rule 17.
Always look at the big picture

One of the things that differentiates high fliers in a business from their management colleagues is the size and scope of their thinking. People who look beyond the details of a problem to see the long-term implications and who learn to place issues within a wider strategic context will always be seen as people with potential for higher level roles.

They may not always be more clever or more competent than their colleagues, but because they have wider thinking horizons they will be able to increase their value to their current organisation and will be able to make a more broadly based contribution to its long-term development.

Broadening your horizons and thinking beyond the norm is an important habit to develop. It raises your profile with important opinion formers and leads to greater levels of influence within your organisation or your profession. Read biographies of business or political leaders and you will see that their career growth has normally been characterised by making bold and unconventional moves rather than conforming to organisational norms.

Actions

- Examine your career goals – are they ambitious or cautious? Think beyond your current reality into a wider perspective.
- Find out about your organisation's

strategy. How can you make changes in
your job to better support this strategy?

Rule 18.
Keep things simple

Many people have discovered that trying to
'do it all' or to 'have it all' means having less
and less as they begin to feel overwhelmed by
the vast range of things available to them. We
live in a complex world, faced with masses of
information and many choices, each one as
tempting or interesting as the next. We can't
have or do it all and so we must try to simplify
our working lives to focus on those things
which give us the best return for our time.

This means having a simple personal organisation system, it means focusing on the critical drivers of performance or career growth,
learning to say no to 'nice to do' projects, and
it requires setting some priorities and focusing
on them, while ruthlessly pruning out the
'administrivia' (paper and e-mails).

Actions

- Examine your activities at work and at
  home. Are they taking you towards your
  career goals? If they aren't, think of ways
  to stop doing them. Prune timewasters
  ruthlessly in order to focus on the really
  important features of your work and your
  life outside work.
- Conduct a major review of your papers
  and possessions. Throw away things that
  are no longer useful and that you are
  keeping 'just in case' – that goes for

books you won't read again, clothes you
won't wear again and files that you won't
use again.
- Identify the 'critical few' projects that will
give you the best returns in terms of
contribution to the organisation and your
own personal development.

Rule 19.

**To make progress, keep your skills up to
date**

As the challenges in your industry or business
grow, you will need to widen your set of skills
to ensure that you remain successful.

There are three broad skill areas that most
professionals and managers need to keep
themselves fully effective: professional/techni-
cal, business, and personal competencies. All
three skill clusters need to be kept up to date if
you are going to achieve career success.

Actions

- Put a development plan in place
  immediately to enable you to keep your
  skills up to date.
- Start up a learning log to capture
  important learning points from activities
  at work and at home. Write down your
  goals and general thoughts about your
  career and your personal development.
- Talk to your training and development
  manager about available development
  programmes within your organisation.
  Don't go on a course just because it's
  there; find a programme that meets your
  needs and your personal learning style.

Rule 20.

Make career management a life-long habit for life-long success

Most people only analyse their career options and review their strengths and weaknesses when they have been made redundant – when it is often too late. Managing your career is a life-long process; you should be constantly keeping your skills up to date, reviewing your goals and taking stock of where you want to be in the future. This should start from your first assignment and go on until and beyond when you receive your gold clock – even in retirement, we should still be seeking out new goals and learning new skills.

Actions

- Keep working at your career development.
- Clarify what you want to achieve and then develop strategies and skills to help you achieve it.
- Review your progress and reset your goals when you find they have been achieved or when the world changes and you need to rethink your career development.

....

SUMMARY

Career management benefits both the individual and the organisation. It is a working life-long process that should help you enjoy your work and gain satisfaction and other rewards from it. This in turn will improve your personal life, for the two must be managed side by side.

Plan Your Career has taken you through the processes for starting to plan and manage your career. Now you must keep it up! The twenty rules expanded on in the text and summarised in this chapter should help you keep on track. Remember that plans change as circumstances change, and the suggested actions given here will provide guidance on updating your plans.

REFERENCES AND FURTHER READING

Covey, Stephen, *First Things First*, Simon & Schuster, 1994

Covey, Stephen, *The Seven Habits of Highly Effective People*, Simon & Schuster, 1992

de Bono, Edward, *Six Thinking Hats*, Penguin, 1985

De Geus, Arie, *The Living Company*, Nicholas Brealey, 1997

Descartes, *Discourses on Method*

Fassell, Diane, *Working Ourselves to Death*, Thorsons, 1990

Handy, Charles, *The Empty Raincoat*, Random House, 1994

Handy, Charles, *In Search of Meaning*, Random House, 1996

Heir, Ben, *The Professional Decision Thinker*, Sidgewick & Jackson, 1986

Hopkins, Tom, *The Official Guide to Success*, HarperCollins, 1994

Kinsman, Francis, *Millennium*, Penguin, 1990

McDonald, Malcolm, *Marketing Plans*, Butterworth-Heinemann, 1984

McRae, Hamish, *The World in 2020*, HarperCollins, 1994

Moss Kanter, Rosabeth, *When Giants Learn to Dance*, Simon & Schuster, 1989

Naisbett, John, *Global Paradox*, Nicholas Brealey, 1994

Naisbett, John, *Megatrends 2000*, Sidgewick & Jackson, 1990

Popcorn, Faith, *Clicking*, HarperCollins, 1996

Schwarz, Peter, *The Art of the Long View*, Century Business, 1991

Spear, William, *Feng Shui Made Easy*, HarperCollins, 1995

Wilson Shaef, Anne and Fassell, Diane, *The Addictive Organisation*, Harper and Row, 1998

INDEX